Gender in Development Organisations

Edited by Caroline Sweetman

Oxfam

The books in Oxfam's *Focus on Gender* series were originally published as single issues of the journal *Gender and Development* (formerly *Focus on Gender*). *Gender and Development* is published by Oxfam three times a year. It is the only British journal to focus specifically on gender and development issues internationally, to explore the links between gender and development initiatives, and to make the links between theoretical and practical work in this field. For information about subscription rates, please apply to Carfax Publishing Company, PO Box 25, Abingdon, Oxfordshire OX14 3UE, UK; Fax: +44 (0) 1235 401550. In North America, please apply to Carfax Publishing Company, 875-81 Massachusetts Avenue, Cambridge, MA 02139; Fax: (+1) 617 354 6875. In Australia, please apply to Carfax Publishing Company, PO Box 352, Cammeray, NSW 2062, Australia; Fax: +61 (0) 2 9958 2376.

Practical Action Publishing Ltd
25 Albert Street, Rugby, CV21 2SD, Warwickshire, UK
www.practicalactionpublishing.com

First published by Oxfam 1997. Reprinted by Oxfam GB in 1999
Reprinted by Practical Action Publishing
Converted to digital file 2010

© Oxfam(UK and Ireland) 1997

Oxfam GB is registered as a charity in England and Wales (no. 202918) and
Scotland (SCO 039042).
Oxfam GB is a member of Oxfam International.

Paperback ISBN: 9780855983659
PDF ISBN: 9780855987497

A catalogue record for this publication is available from the British Library.

Front cover: *A trainee community healthworker leads a discussion on
household hygine during a worksop held near Bukumbi, Tanzania.*
Photo: *Geoff Sayer*

Contents

Editorial

Organisations are culturally-defined entities, which reflect and replicate the values of those who set them up: 'national cultural values are reflected in the ways organisations function, and these values stereotype appropriate roles and behaviours in ways that generally limit women's access to resources and decision-making' (Anderson 1993). This collection of articles examines these issues in the context of development organisations; looking at organisations as social mechanisms in this way makes examining gender and organisational culture of central relevance to development practitioners and policy-makers.

A crucial question is what the term 'gender equity' means to different stakeholders. For some, taking on a commitment to this goal may mean no more than the adoption of an equal opportunities policy. For others, it means targeting women as beneficiaries in development interventions. For a third group, a concern for gender equity means adopting a radical political agenda which asserts not only women's needs, but their rights to full participation in decision-making at all levels. In this light, taking on a 'gender agenda' has implications for the internal running of development organisations as well as for the development interventions they undertake.

All the authors in this collection emphasise the interlinkedness of the external and internal contexts for development organisations. No longer is it tenable to see interventions as existing in 'the field', divorced from the guiding principles which have formed the organisation's purpose and structure, and determined the choice of staff. Working on gender issues obliges organisations to set their own houses in order, and change aspects of the organisational culture which discriminate against women staff, and women 'beneficiaries'.

Gender and organisations: a three-dimensional view

Gender in the context of development organisations is a complex topic. In this introduction, the articles to follow are contextualised through the use of an analytical framework which highlights the inter-relationship between the cultural and structural elements of organisations. The framework, originally developed by Marge Schuler to analyse the law and legal systems, emphasises the importance of considering three interdependent elements: the substantive (laws, or organ-isational policies); the structural (procedures and mechanisms to enforce the substantive level); and the cultural (beliefs and attitudes held by wider society, including the women and men who work in the organisation).[1] But while Schuler's framework may be of use in discussing why and how development agencies have worked on gender issues, artificially distinguishing between the elements in this way is only helpful if we remain clear that, ultimately, the topic needs to be considered holistically.

The substantive level: reaching a shared vision

If gender and development has moved from the fringe to the mainstream of development, this should be cause for celebration rather than the feeling of unease about what has been lost in the translation (Jackson 1996, 489).

Examining the substantive level of organisations, as defined in their mandate and objectives, can explain why in some organisations, gender issues have been 'depoliticised' to fit into a conservative or liberal world-view rather than a radical agenda of social transformation.

Recently, gender and development researchers have questioned an apparent consensus around the objectives of gender equality and social transformation (Jahan 1995) which exists between very different types of development organisation. They have found that this common professional language cloaks a very wide range of ideological standpoints. Radical messages about gender equity have been 'translated' into policies with more conservative rationales and goals: an obvious example is the widespread use of the term 'empowerment' by feminist activists and multilateral aid agencies alike (Rowlands 1997). Grassroots women and feminist activists (both inside and outside

mainstream[2] development organisations) share a common vocabulary with each other and with practitioners and policy-makers in organisations which have grafted a commitment to working to promote gender equity onto a markedly different root-stock.

Tensions which exist between very different constituencies in development are more easily addressed if there is clarity on the fact that we do not all mean the same thing when we speak of 'doing gender'. For example, awareness of the different agendas which underlie the rhetoric of 'gender' aids understanding of instances where 'unplanned' outcomes may be dismissed as 'project misbehaviour' (Buvinic 1986).

Women as instruments: WID approaches
In her 1995 study of the way four bilateral development donor agencies have handled gender issues, Rounaq Jahan found that 'the relationship between WID/GAD policy objectives and the agency and governments' overall objectives was not clear' (Jahan 1995, 115). The idea that gender relations are fundamentally concerned with power has been conspicuously absent from much of the WID/GAD literature emanating from these agencies (White 1992). It therefore appears that, consciously or unconsciously, mainstream development organisations have 'bypassed a large part of the women's agenda' (ibid., 4).

There are two notable features at the substantive level of mainstream development organisations. First, most have a mandate based on their history of working to eradicate economic poverty in a post-war, post-colonial context; they do not inherently question the assumption that the world should 'develop' along Western lines. During the International Decade for Women 1976-85, most development agencies which adopted a WID perspective did so from a growing awareness of women's marginalisation from development activity and their potential in contributing to economic growth (Kabeer 1994). Attempts to integrate women into existing economic, social and political structures were due to a recognition of their potential force in driving forward development along Western lines. This is an argument based on a rationale of efficiency rather than equality. Women are reduced to an instrumental role in delivering a Eurocentric, male-dominated vision of development.

The second feature of the substantive level of mainstream organisations — including international and national government structures — is that the majority are rooted in a bureaucratic ideal of organisations as culture-free. Weber's classic model of the 'ideal-type' of bureaucratic government characterises bureaucracies as a neutral space, where impartial decision-making is based on a clear system of adherence to rules based on rationality (Gerhardi, 1995). However, bureaucracies have a very distinct culture, founded on Western values rooted in the nineteenth century, which emphasises 'the separation of the public realm of rationality from the private one of emotionality and private feelings' (ibid, 45). Much writing on gender issues in organisations chooses to characterise this separation as 'masculine',[3] reflecting the norm of a male workforce which is not primarily responsible for reproductive duties including child-care.

Women as 'the poorest of the poor'

Organisations (including many NGOs) which offer a critique of existing development models have typically taken on gender issues through adapting their organisational purpose to challenge gender aspects of power relations in a given social context. In the case of Oxfam UK/Ireland, a gender policy for the organisation was ratified in 1993 on the grounds that 'Oxfam believes that unless gender-related inequalities are addressed, it will not be possible to achieve sustainable development and alleviate poverty' (Oxfam 1993, 2). Poverty here is defined more widely, including a distancing from political, social and economic power.

Yet, while a broad definition of poverty such as this can offer a rationale for working on gender issues, unequal power relations between women and men *per se* are not brought into question by a mandate to work on poverty alleviation (Jackson 1996). While it is essential to bring a gender perspective to anti-poverty programmes, there are forms of gender-based subordination which fall beyond the bounds of anti-poverty programmes. In this sense, equating anti-poverty goals with those of gender equity ultimately weakens women's claim to equality on grounds of justice (ibid).

Transformation and alternative visions

While mainstream development agencies themselves may see their WID/GAD activities as being part of the solution, many Southern — and Northern — women activists see them as forming part of the problem (DAWN 1989). In comparison, organisations which are founded on a feminist goal of 'structural transformation' (Dakar Declaration of Another Development with Women 1982, quoted in Jahan 1995) aim to promote gender equity as a goal in itself, together with a radical alternative vision of society and development.

In this issue, Hope Chigudu discusses the vision of alternative development that lies at the heart of feminist organisations. In comparison with the bureaucratic ideal of organisations as a value-free zone, this vision is of organisations as part of a wider movement for social change. The public and private divide is therefore not only a false distinction, but is actually undesirable. Organisations should value qualities associated with the private sphere and with femininity – for example, empathy and nurturing – within the workplace.

The patriarchal principles on which many organisations are based are particularly evident in those which provide institutional care for children. Elizabeth Everett explores the efforts of Lesotho Save the Children to integrate gender sensitivity into its work.

The structural level: words into action

The majority of articles in this issue reflect the current focus by researchers and practitioners on the structural level of organisations: the procedures, activities and regulations which translate an organisation's purpose into outcomes.

A decade ago, much emphasis was placed on the importance of placing gender on the organisational agenda. Once the principles were in place, the next common step was working on what Schuler calls the 'cultural level': consciousness-raising of staff through gender training 'in both the community and development organisations' (Murthy forthcoming). Yet this process has not proved adequate. Social transformation in organisations can be de-railed at the structural level: verbal and paper commitments to a vision of gender equity have a tendency to 'evaporate' when there is resistance to putting policy into practice through the procedures, mechanisms and rules of the organisation (Longwe 1995). Feminists need to understand and combat such 'evaporation'. Angela Hadjipateras' article in this collection provides a case study of ACORD, one of many organisations which adopted a policy on gender as 'a statement of goals and principles', but without the clear guidelines which are needed to implement the policy.

An essential part of these guidelines are gender-sensitive instruments to measure women's development; Shalendra Sharma's article highlights this in the context of the Human Development Index (HDI).

In her article, Randa Husseini discusses UNIFEM's experience of working with government and NGOs to promote women's entrepreneurship. Here again, the lack of gender-sensitive data was a major obstacle.

An interesting line of enquiry is whether the organisational structures of development organisations are actually more 'woman-friendly' than those of organisations in the private sector. While at the substantive level, development agencies which question current norms of development may be more receptive to challenging gender stereotyping and women's subordination, paradoxically, the structural level may actually be less friendly to carers. Career development may be virtually impossible for women and men with caring responsibilities, because of the long working hours and prolonged and frequent travel which is expected of senior staff. Additional moral pressure to overwork can be experienced by staff in organisations which have a commitment to 'changing the world' (personal communication, Oxfam 1996).

Mainstream organisational structures
Mainstream organisational structures reveal their bureaucratic origins, where 'everyday work patterns came to be structured around [men's] physical needs and capabilities — in particular, their capacity to achieve relative liberation from child care and domestic responsibilities' (Goetz 1995, 5).

In her article, Anne Marie Goetz discusses the ways in which organisational structures include what she terms 'gendered patterns of space and time', focusing on the Bangladesh NGO, BRAC. She asserts that in order to achieve the goal of gender equity in organisations, radical change is needed to create work-places and working conditions which are friendly to women.

There are a number of dimensions to this. In practical terms, women's responsibility as primary carers for their families means that employers must consider how to respect this role and make it possible to balance reproductive responsibilities with formal employment (Legum 1996). It is now a truism that the goal of gender equality within organisational structures will not occur unless organisations understand that employees have rights and responsibilities as carers.

Yet, while it is true that in most societies it is far more likely that women will be found in the role of primary carers, to equate women with carers is inaccurate, misleading, and counterproductive; the terms are not synonymous with each other. Conflating them has important negative implications for male carers, and women who are not mothers.

This distinction has important implications. First, distinguishing women from carers firstly confirms women as human beings in their own right, by questioning the way in which they are commonly defined through their relations with others. Discrimination on grounds of gender also operates at an ideological level. Implying that the *only* obstacle to women's complete equality with men in organisations is their role as carers is misleading since it wrongly identifies the sexual division of labour as the basis of beliefs about women's inferiority to men. In fact, the relationship is more complex: 'the roles played by men and women are ... determined by culture and by socio-political and economic factors' (Brett 1991, 4). Thus, single women or married women without dependents will still experience gender discrimination in the workplace.

Secondly, making such a distinction demonstrates that debates about perinatal leave and leave to care for sick children should not focus only on women; instead, supportive structures are needed for all carers, regardless of their sex.

Creating woman-friendly organisational structures

It would be rash to condemn all aspects of the bureaucratic model of organisations as intrinsically opposed to a social transformation agenda. Yet, the more existing development models are questioned by non-profit organisations, the more likely it is they will reject the conventional bureaucratic structure of administration for these models.

For women's organisations, a commitment to challenging hierarchical, male-dominated decision-making may lead to a rejection of pyramidal power relations, in favour of co-operative ways of working: 'the core assumption [is] that if women are to succeed in making fundamental change then they must by definition choose fundamentally different, i.e. non-hierarchical, democratic modes for organisation' (Stewart and Taylor 1995, 80).

In her article, Hope Chigudu points out that the pressures on organisations promoting alternative values in the workplace are typically exacerbated by the imbalances in power relationships between donor agencies and women's organisations in developing countries. Organisations are faced by the challenge of balancing a commitment to an alternative vision with meeting requirements for funding, in an unequal 'partnership' between a bureaucratic donor and a feminist counterpart agency. The difficulty and stresses presented by living out alternative values, in an external context which is invariably inhospitable, means many women activists simply 'burn-out'.

Similar pressures to conform to patriarchal values are shared by the 'cells' of feminist activists — or 'change agents' — in the WID/GAD teams of mainstream organisations. In their article, Rieky Stuart and Aruna Rao discuss the role of the change agent. In her study mentioned previously, Rounaq Jahan found staff leading a schizophrenic existence: 'to succeed inside, [staff] needed to fit into the organisational mould and play by the rules; to succeed outside, they needed to challenge the organisation and change the rules' (Jahan 1995, 119).

The cultural level: hearts as well as minds?

The role of change agents in challenging organisations to turn rhetoric on gender issues into reality brings us to consider the third aspect of Schuler's framework: the cultural element, consisting of the beliefs and attitudes of the individuals involved in the work. This emphasises the power of people to facilitate or impede organisational change.

The close association of women with culture may mean that introducing a commitment to working towards gender equity at the substantive level, and methods of working which challenge norms of female behaviour at the structural level, takes not only commitment, but considerable courage on the part of female staff. 'it is an acknowledged factor that in nearly all civilisations women have been viewed as "guardians of culture"' (Dawit and Busia 1995, 9). In her article, Anne Marie Goetz explores the experience of female employees working for an organisation with a vision of social transformation including gender equity.

There is considerable evidence that taking on an organisational commitment to gender equity will become reality only if staff 'own' it. The fact that we are all assigned a gender — however we define sex and gender, and the relationship between these terms — means we all approach the issues from a perspective of knowledge. Our personal experience informs our receptivity to working on gender issues, and the way we choose to engage with them; organisations may tolerate resistance on grounds of personal experience where such reasoning would not be seen as acceptable on other issues concerned with diversity, such as race (Staudt 1991).

Challenging the private/public divide between who we are and what we do, in a process of conscientisation, has therefore been seen as a central activity by development agencies (Murthy, forthcoming). Strategies have evolved to bring about attitudinal change on the part of staff, including gender training: 'rather than promoting a mechanical implementation of gender-equitable development, gender training aims to develop thought and action in a transformational manner' (Williams et al. 1995, xi).

It is important to recognise the likely existence of 'sub-cultures' and 'counter-cultures' in organisations (Staudt 1991); while the public face of the organisation may appear monolithic, groups of individuals who do not completely identify with the ruling culture will nevertheless exist. Efforts to integrate gender into the organisation need to take into account the opportunities — and the constraints — offered by engagement with these other cultures. In her article focusing on AFRA in South Africa, Moya Bydawell discusses issues that arose for the organisation when its gender training activities addressed resistance from some staff to working on gender issues, on grounds that gender issues were challenging to black South African culture.

Just as work on gender has been taken on more easily, and at a more challenging level, by organisations whose aim is social transformation, the staff of these organisations may already be attuned to taking on gender issues, seeing themselves as part of a 'social movement' (personal communication). Yet ironically, it is the staff of organisations with a non-conformist tradition, allied to a liberal world-view, who may find it most difficult to accept that organisational imperatives may require individuals to internalise new values imposed from above, in order to perform their roles.

Present crises and future directions

If donors and their development partners were able to stay with other issues such as population and poverty alleviation for several decades ... why [are] they becoming impatient with WID results? (Jahan 1995, 11)

Working to promote equality between women and men is a lengthy, complex process, particularly because of the issues of gender-differentiated power. Reluctant to take on the radical goal of social transformation with equality between women and men, some mainstream development agencies are showing signs of 'WID fatigue' (ibid.) despite the short time spent thus far in focusing on gender issues in development. Gender may be dismissed in an era of 'post-feminism', or seen as yesterday's fad — a priority which should now be replaced by a new commitment. This has serious implications for mainstream development organisations themselves, and for the work they perform in partnership with feminist organisations in South and North.

Resource constraints provide a convenient pretext for mainstream agencies to strengthen the arguments rehearsed above, and place additional pressure on organisations working towards social transformation along feminist lines. How can gender issues be placed, and kept, at the centre of 'good development' at a time when public and private funds for development initiatives are under threat? Funding for innovative work on gender issues is increasingly scarce, as donor agencies shift the terms of their debates to the language of welfare and 'basic needs' (personal communication, 1996). Yet, as gender and development practitioners and activists have asserted, women's needs and rights are interlinked (Facio 1995); political commitment and sound gender analysis are essential elements for development policy and planning. Good development work is good gender work.

In turning the rhetoric of gender equity into the reality of a radical agenda of transformation in all aspects of relations between the sexes, recognition must be given to the value of alliances between stakeholders who have different identities, but agree to work towards a common aim (Theobald 1996). Building on diverse identities and experience is a positive way of harnessing the strengths of women and men, and of theorists and practitioners, who may be located in different types of organisation within various economic, political and cultural contexts.

Networking and linking increase the impact of work at community and national level, through influencing change at macro-level; an example is 'Women's Eyes on the Bank', a lobbying initiative set up at Beijing. Lastly, the position and status of 'change agents' within organisations is critical, if they are to be empowered to challenge dominant ideologies of gender relations within a hierarchical organisation, and keep up the momentum for positive transformation.

References

Anderson, M (1993) 'The concept of mainstreaming: experience and change' in Anderson, M (ed) *Focusing on Women: UNIFEM's Experience in Mainstreaming*, UNIFEM: New York.

Brett, A (1991) 'Why gender is a development issue' in *Changing Perceptions: Writings on Gender and Development*, Oxfam, Oxford.

Buvinic, M (1986) 'Projects for women in the Third World: explaining their misbehaviour', *World Development* 14: 5.

Dawit, S and Busia, A (1995) 'Thinking about "culture"; some programme pointers', *Gender and Development* 3: 1.

DAWN (1989) 'Women in Development', Paper presented at XVth Annual General Assembly of Development Non-Governmental organisations, Bruissels, April 18-21, 1989.

Facio, A (1995) 'From basic needs to basic rights', *Gender and Development*, 3:2.

Gerhardi, S (1995) *Gender, Symbolism and Organisational Cultures*, Sage: London.

Goetz, A–M (1995) 'Institutionalising women's interests and gender-sensitive accountability in development', *IDS Bulletin* 26: 3 *Getting Institutions Right for Women in Development* IDS: Sussex.

Jackson, C (1996) 'Rescuing gender from the poverty trap', *World Development* 24: 3.

Jahan, R (1995) *The Elusive Agenda: Mainstreaming Women in Development* Zed Books: London.

Kabeer, N (1994) *Reversed Realities*, Verso.

Legum, M (1996) 'The right time to institutionalise gender', mimeo.

Longwe, S (1995) 'A development agency as a patriarchal cooking pot: the evaporation of policies for women's advancement' in Macdonald M. (ed) *Women's Rights and Development: Vision and Strategy for the Twenty-first Century*, Oxfam Discussion Paper 6, Oxfam: UK.

Moser, C and Levy, C 'A theory and methodology of gender planning: meeting women's practical and strategic needs', mimeo.

Murthy, R K 'Towards gender-transformative training: lessons from South Asia' in *Gender Training: The Source Book* (provisional title), *Critical Reviews and Annotated Bibliographies* 2, KIT Publications, forthcoming.

Nicholson, P (1996) *Gender, Power and Organisation: A Psychological Perspective*, Routledge: London.

Oxfam UK/Ireland (1993) 'Gender and development: Oxfam's policy for its programme', internal document.

Staudt, K (1991) *Managing Development: State, Society, and International Contexts* Sage: London.

Stewart, S and Taylor, J (1995) 'Women organising women: doing it backwards and in high heels' in *IDS Bulletin 26:3 Getting institutions right for women in development* IDS: Sussex.

Theobald, S (1996) 'Employment and industrial hazard: women workers and strategies of resistance in northern Thailand', *Gender and Development* 4: 3.

White, S (1992) *Arguing with the Crocodile: Gender and Class in Bangladesh* Zed Books: London.

Williams, S, Seed, J and Mwau, A (1995) *The Oxfam Gender Training Manual*, Oxfam, Oxford.

Notes

1 The links between these three elements are complex; listing them in the order given here does not imply that one of them comes first, or is more important than the others.

2 Defined here as national, bilateral and multilateral level organisations: including both government organisations and NGOs.

3 However, labelling particular qualities as intrinsically 'masculine' or 'feminine' is seen as by Paula Nicholson, a feminist psychologist, as a limiting view of gender identity in the workplace (Nicholson 1996)

Rethinking organisations:

a feminist perspective

Aruna Rao and Rieky Stuart

In April 1996, 24 women and men from Asia, Africa, Latin and North America, and Europe met for five days in Canada, to share their experience of helping organisations, especially development organisations, to include women in their programmes, and ensure equitable power relations between women and men. This article gives an account of some of the ideas and observations about organisational transformation which emerged at this conference.

In the past few years, those of us who work in development organisations have seen a number of brilliant and extremely useful efforts by individuals, both women and men, which have made a difference for women. Each of us could identify programmes, projects, and initiatives that have been quite stunning in their impact. But our impression is that these successes, important as they are, have mainly been accomplished by individuals who are often swimming against the flow in their own organisation. They succeed in spite of, and not because of, the way their organisations work.

The writers of this article chose organisational transformation as a focus for the Canada conference, and for our wider work, because organisations are such important arenas of human engagement. Whether they are small NGOs, government departments, universities, or for-profit companies, organisations are fundamental features of our societies, and very important ways of mobilising social energy. We need to think more deeply about organisations themselves. Trying to 'add gender' into their structure and work is not enough; we need to understand and re-conceptualise what an organisation is, and then we need to re-invent organisations and institutions of all kinds in all our societies.

It became clear at the conference that what we are aiming at is organisational *transformation*. We are not talking about organisational development, nor about organisational change. In the case of development organisations, we mean including women as architects and designers of programmes, and as agents, managers, and beneficiaries; and reshaping social institutions and organisations to include men and women's varied perspectives.[1] We want to move organisations in a direction that can accommodate, cherish, and foster the creativity and the productivity of women, men, young, old, people of colour, people of differing ability. We want organisations to incorporate goals and values that are life-affirming, human-centred, and justice-oriented. We need to challenge and change the 'deep structures' of the organisations in which we work.

Theory and methodology

There are two conceptual 'lenses' that we have found very useful in our work, both theoretically and practically. One is organisational theory. There is a body of knowledge about what organisations are, how they work, and how they change, that has not been generally incorporated by development practitioners, including gender and development practitioners.

The second conceptual lens is more familiar: the learning from feminist theory and practice, from Women in Development (WID) initiatives, and the learning from attempts to apply a gender perspective to development. Using these two lenses together is very helpful in identifying promising approaches to organisational transformation.

Images of organisations

At the Canada conference, we began by asking people to share with us their images of and metaphors for organisations. We wanted them to think holistically about what an organisation is.

Organisations as onions
We ourselves have worked with a very wide range of development and other organisations, including Northern and Southern NGOs, bilateral and multilateral organisations, and for-profit organisations. The image that captures our experience of introducing a gender perspective in organisations is the peeling of an onion. An onion must be peeled to release its flavour, yet the process brings tears; and

as you peel, you encounter layer after layer. Recognising that organisations, too, have many 'layers', helps to explain why strategies and activities focused on a single layer of the organisation may be necessary but may not be sufficient.

For example, one of the approaches to change in organisations is by developing gender policies. Sometimes the policies look marvellous, and are very useful for public relations purposes. But often they don't have many plans or resources attached to them; they sit and gather dust on the shelves. A policy on affirmative action is necessary, but not sufficient. The actual number of women, or old people, or young people, or people of colour in an organisation is important but more important is how they think and what they do. Gender parity and meeting diversity quotas may not change power relations which are structured by gender, race or class.

Similarly, initiatives which address a single aspect of the ways in which the organisation fails to consider women are necessary but not sufficient. Simply performing a gender analysis is not enough. We can know how women in general or specific groups of women are disadvantaged, in the organisation itself and in its work, but if we lack the capacity to change the situation, organisational transformation will not occur.

A third example is the use of performance indicators. These, too, are necessary but not sufficient, if performance is measured solely in terms of counting inputs, and does not focus on outcomes or impact. One of the famous jokes at Canadian CIDA is the response of some engineers when asked about the differential impact of their highway construction project on women and men: 'well, women walk on roads too' (personal communication). Even gender training and sensitisation are necessary but not sufficient, if participants are unable or unwilling to apply their learning.

Organisations as icebergs

Another participant thought of organisations as icebergs: when you study an organisation, you may not see all that exists. Each organisation has unconscious or submerged values in its culture, and a history which influences its way of working. These unseen dimensions may move an organisation in a direction which you may not anticipate, if all you consider is what can be seen on the surface. In our discussions, we termed that which is not visible, 'deep structure'. In trying to transform organisations, we need to be more aware of what is unconscious or invisible, and what is conscious or visible, to resolve the tensions between the two.

Our first illustration of this comes from the findings of some work done in for-profit corporations in the US (Rapoport et al., forthcoming). This Ford Foundation-supported action-research carried out in three sites within the Xerox Corporation, Corning, and Tandem Corporations, used a work-family lens to introduce workplace innovations that helped to ease the personal situation of the employees while at the same time enhancing business goals. The research revealed that one set of characteristics and behaviour that was unconsciously valued in these organisations was heroism. A 'hero' — someone who will stay at the office working for 24 hours when the report is due, who can respond to an emergency and solve the problem — is noticed, has a high profile, feels valued, and is promoted.

In comparison, the report showed that skills such as preventing crises, building relationships, coordinating, thinking in advance, and helping things to move smoothly and calmly, were effectively invisible; they were undervalued, and not as likely to lead to promotion. The unconscious values, which reinforce 'heroic' behaviour and make the exercise of preventive skills invisible, are one example of what we called 'deep structure'.

Another example was given by a participant at the Canada conference. She told fellow participants that in her view, the visible purpose of the World Bank is development. But what is unacknowledged, is that the really important task is to move money — lots of it — on time. This is what people are rewarded for. Moving money on time and in big quantities may or may not be good development. There are tensions on many levels, including the amount of money that the multilateral agency thinks is appropriate to lend to a particular country, and the many definitions of 'good development' on the part of lender, beneficiary government, and NGOs of all kinds within the country (Conference, 1995).

A third example of the need to consider the deep structure of an organisation comes from the work we have been doing with BRAC, the well-known NGO in Bangladesh. A central goal of BRAC is the empowerment of the disadvantaged, particularly poor women. One of the ways this is put into practice is through a credit programme. The staff spend a lot of time giving out loans and collecting loan instalments, and this may occasionally be done quite coercively; coercion of poor women to make repayments is hardly empowerment. Thus, there is a tension between the espoused goals and values of the organisation and its way of working (personal experience, BRAC Gender Team, August 1996).

Focusing on three areas of deep structure

There are three areas of deep structure that participants believed to be of particular importance in looking at gender and organisational transformation.

The 'work:life' divide

First, in almost all organisations there is a dichotomy between paid work and everything else: family, community, life. Work is extremely important, both in the amount of time allocated to paid work, and in the meaning and shape it gives to people's lives. This is an aspect of modernisation that seems inseparable from organisations as we know them.

When we are at work, we are not supposed to be concerned with family or with community. When we look at an organisation's practice, we need to pay attention to evidence of expectations that staff should place their employment at the centre of their lives. This is very significant when trying to address gender inequality, because of women's current role as primary carers for the family.

The exercise of power

A second area of deep structure to look for concerns the practice of power. In almost all organisations, power is equated with control and hierarchy. One metaphor for this is to think of power as a pie: if I have more, you have less. The superior takes as much of the pie as he or she can get, and the subordinate has to be satisfied with less.

In examining this aspect of deep structure, one of the characteristics to look for is who has the information and how it is shared; organisations can spend a great deal of time worrying about information, because it is a source of power.

A different way of thinking about power is as something we can create, add to, and build on. Instead of seeing power as a finite resource, power is infinite. For example, parents have almost complete power over their small children. Parents do not necessarily feel, as the child grows up and becomes more powerful, that they become less powerful. If their goal is to raise children who are strong, independent, responsible, and capable, then accomplishing this enhances the parents' own social power and prestige. This view of power stresses it as a source of energy,

which has to be distributed to be useful: a very different view from that prevalent in most organisations; however, some use this understanding of power when they talk about 'self-managing teams', or about 'mentoring'.

Foci and ways of working

A third area of organisational deep structure is what we are tentatively calling the 'monoculture of instrumentality'. What we mean by this phrase is the tendency of organisations to focus narrowly on a single purpose, and on one course of action to get there. These limited objectives, ways of working, and perceptions are often indicated by the presence of departmental 'silos' which try to exist as independently as possible. For example, in BRAC, we might say that the 'monoculture' of credit and meeting credit targets drives out an attention to broader aspects of women's empowerment. Yet achieving credit targets is not the only way to foster women's empowerment.

To have more complex objectives for organisations is more challenging but also richer. A corporation normally has one goal: to earn profit. Adding to that the goals of being a good corporate citizen, a good employer, and environmentally sound, greatly complicates how that organisation works. But it may also make it richer in many dimensions, including its long-term profitability. Attention to the balance between family and work, in the Ford Foundation study, for example, also resulted in increased productivity in several cases.

Another aspect of monocultural thinking is that rationality is the only aspect of human intellect which is appropriate to the workplace. In fact, people in organisations do not operate only on the basis of intellect, but on intuition, emotions, the ego, and complex individual needs.

While the visible structure uses the language of intellect, merit, and accomplishment for all organisational processes and products, what may actually be driving decisions and actions are emotions and needs such as the desire for status and power.

Finally, if an organisation thinks too narrowly or instrumentally about accomplishing stated goals, it may undermine its ability to achieve those goals. Even if organisations believe, for example, that diversity of thought and equity among different groups represented on the staff enrich the organisation, they often also fear that such diversity is costly. That cost they see as a distraction from the main enterprise of the organisation. What they do not often see is the reward: greater resources and perspectives to tap in order to cope with external change and tackle internal problems.

Promoting change in the deep structure

Participants at the Conference had various ideas about approaches that had the potential to change aspects of the deep structure of organisations, in terms of gender issues:

Linking feminist goals to organisational values

First, the feminist goals of social transformation need to be linked to the espoused values of the organisation. Positive change will not come about if there is no direct connection between women's empowerment, gender transformation, and the explicit values of the organisation. For example, in BRAC, the Gender Programme focused on the organisation's goal of poverty alleviation and women's empowerment by working on programme and organisational quality. This meant addressing a range of issues concerning programme effectiveness, organisational systems and cultures, and the ability of the organisation to retain greater numbers of qualified women staff, as well as fostering better working relationships between male and female staff.

If, however, an intervention is linked solely to the narrower objectives of an organisation — effectiveness of the credit programme, for example — there may be very real short-term gains, but there is a danger in the long run that the goal of gender equity will be disregarded because it is not congruent with the real business of the organisation. Most if not all not-for-profit institutions have socially laudable goals. Therefore, linking these goals with gender equity objectives becomes a matter of judgement and creativity on the part of the change agent, who needs to use a variety of strategies to build support for organisational transformation. Organisations which are not run for profit may couch their motivations in language which suggests a commitment to social transformation; this potentially provides a lever with which to work.

Understanding multiple perspectives

Secondly, it is critical to start from where people are. Strategies must be negotiated, and spaces for change must be sought. We are all familiar with the multiple meanings attached to the concept of 'gender', and the many implications of these for different organisational contexts, and for different people. We must negotiate with members of the organisations, and discover what they see the issues to be regarding gender.

There will be a variety of factors to consider: where to start, what level on which to begin work, which strategies might work, and what needs to be negotiated with the various groups involved. Clearly, elegant formulations and theories of gender relations and women's disadvantage (even useful ones), may need to be modified to focus on the particular requirements of the organisational context.

However, negotiation is not simply a tactic to increase the enthusiasm of those with whom one is engaging in the organisations; the ideas of the change agent are also a subject for negotiation. Though as change agents we need to be clear that we have our own ideals and perspectives, and are speaking in our own voices, we cannot remain fixed in our own position. We are not limited to the role of advocate. We need to be aware in our turn that aspects of deep structure are embedded in our own unconscious; perhaps those very aspects we are trying to change. As Remmy Rikken of the NGO PILIPINA says, 'this is sacred ground, take your shoes off and walk carefully' (conference, 1995). At the Canada conference, we used the term 'chang*ing* agent' to describe this experience.

Organisational work practices
Third, we need to examine organisational work practices. How does the organisation get the job done? What does this tell you about aspects of deep structure? By examining work practices, we can uncover the dissonance between organisational values and culture — such as the ethic of 'hard work' measured in terms of long hours on the job — and organisational practices as they have evolved over time. In tracing the link between practice and values, you may want to keep the values but change the practice; in some cases, you may want to change the values .

For example, in CIMMYT (Centro Internacional de Mejoramiento de Maiz y Trigo), the maize and wheat institute of the CGIAR (Consultative Group on International Agricultural Research) system, fieldwork is highly valued and it is generally assumed that as a scientist you are not doing real scientific work unless you yourself travel up and down frequently to the experimental stations. Sharing such responsibilities with senior technicians, through working in teams,

has been regarded as shirking one's responsibilities. This 'requirement' of the job has dissuaded many women scientists from applying for jobs at CIMMYT, at a time when the organisation is trying to hire and retain more women and also to find new ways of working, for example, by moving from breeding the best crop varieties toward broader community resource-management goals (Merrill Sands, 1996).

Fourthly, it is important to bring silent voices to the 'surface', or conscious level, of the organisation, and recognise that in every organisation there are contesting meanings. Listening to one group of voices within or outside the organisation reveals only one part of the story. As Joyce Fletcher (Conference participant, Northeastern University, Boston) says, listening to hitherto silent voices fills out the picture. It is a little like a kaleidoscope — every time you shake it or change the lens, you see a slightly different configuration of the same elements.

In listening to these other voices, we are bringing in other concepts of the truth, for example, what it feels like to be at variance with the dominant culture. As Barbara Williams (Conference participant, private consultant working with the City of Toronto) says, we can think of power as circulating in language, and in the knowledge that language authorises. Then it is possible to see gaps in power, complications, and contradictions. Other possibilities for mapping specific organisational processes might be re-envisioned. But this is tricky, because of the power of legitimation: what Stephen Lukes calls the 'power within' — the subordination we accept and internalise without questioning even when it is contrary to our own self-interest (Lukes 1986). Some things are just thought to be right!

Finally, we need to challenge what participants at the Canada Conference termed the 'process-outcome split'. We have a tendency to focus on outcomes rather than process, not recognising that process itself may be an outcome. For example, organisational insiders do not say, 'last year we did accounting, so we don't need to do that any more!' Why should processes of change related to gender be any different? To have an effective organisation, you need to pay attention to accounting all the time. Similarly, you always need to pay attention to gender equity and to deep structure: inherently political processes.

Where does one start? There is an old saying that 'there are no perfect places to start, only real ones'. But each strategy must be grounded in an understanding of deep structure, the importance of the 'work-family split', an understanding of power as control, and the monoculture of instrumentality, to provide pathways for radical change, which is both necessary and sufficient.

Aruna Rao is a gender and development consultant and writer. Editor of 'Women's Studies International: Nairobi and Beyond' *(The Feminist Press, 1991) and* 'Gender Analysis and Development Planning: A Case Book' *(Kumarian Press, 1991), she has written extensively on gender analysis, gender training, and institutional development. From 1994 to 1996, she headed the BRAC Gender Programme. Currently, she is a Visiting Fellow at the Simmons Institute for Leadership and Change in Boston, USA.*

7702 Hamilton Spring Road, Bethesda, MD 20817, USA. tel: 1 301 365 3886; e-mail: rao-kvam@msn.com

Rieky Stuart is Programme Manager for the Canadian Council for International Cooperation, the Canadian umbrella organisation for Canadian development NGOs. A development worker since the 1960s, she has worked as a trainer, writer and consultant on organisational change since 1985.

CCIC, 1 Nicholas Street, Suite 300, ottawa, Ontario K1N 7B7, Canada; tel: 1 613 241 7007; e-mail: ccicpro@web.apc.org

References

Lukes, S (ed) (1986) *Power*, Blackwell: Oxford.

Merrill Sands D Presentation on Gender Issues in the Workplace in CIMMYT at the Association for Women in Development Forum, Washington, DC, September 1996.

Rapoport, R and Bailyn, L (eds) (forthcoming) *Relinking Life and Work: Towards a Better Future*, Ford Foundation, New York.

Notes

1   The report of the conference, *Building a Global Network for Gender and Organizational Change*, by David Kelleher, Aruna Rao, Rieky Stuart and Kirsten Moore can be obtained from Rieky Stuart (CCIC, Ottawa, Canada; tel:1-613-241-7007, extn. 352; fax: 1-613-241-5302; email: ccicpro@web.apc.org

Managing organisational change:

the 'gendered' organisation of space and time

Anne Marie Goetz

This article[1] examines the experiences of women and men staff in the world's largest national NGO, the Bangladesh Rural Advancement Committee (BRAC), to investigate the impact of the organisation of space and time on women's capacity to become effective development workers.

The way development organisations structure everyday work through space (approaches to field work, organisation of office and living space) and through time (structure of the working day, and of the relationship between career and life cycles) reflect the physical and social capabilities of those who dominate organisations. Where an organisation is dominated by men, the institutional time management of working hours, and life cycle career paths can reflect men's relative liberation from child care and domestic responsibilities. This allows them more time for work or institutional interactions beyond the home. They have cultural rights to mobility and autonomy outside the home, and this may be reflected in the organisation's expectations about the amount of travel which employees should undertake.

These practical, everyday aspects of the way organisations structure their work are a feature of the organisation's culture; they will be reflected in performance criteria, rewarding people who flourish within the physical and social (or spatial and temporal) boundaries of the organisation. When organisations take on new participants, such as women staff and women clients, and new objectives, such as promoting women's interests in development, the organisation of space and time can affect the capacity of women staff to compete with men and to become effective development workers.[2] The way these patterns reflect and reproduce the organisation's culture and objectives can affect the capacity of all staff — men and women — to promote gender and development concerns; to work effectively for women's interests.

BRAC maintains a strong commitment to gender equity in its anti-poverty programmes, including an impressive rural credit programme, the Rural Development Programme (RDP), offering credit and income-generating skills and inputs to, at the time of this study, well over 700,000 members, 70 per cent of them women (by 1995 women were 85 per cent of borrowers). Part of BRAC's commitment to gender and development goals is reflected in its efforts to employ women, although there is such a high drop-out rate among women staff that they represent only between 15 and 25 per cent of total staff.

Women staff are in an important and sensitive position in relation to the way BRAC is regarded by village people. In a conservative environment such as rural Bangladesh, the presence of women in non-traditional roles will be particularly noticed and commented upon. This puts rural development organisations which pursue progressive and counter-cultural social goals in a difficult position. In order to accomplish their work, they must respect the social order and cultivate local support. But at the same time, their very presence in rural development work is a symbol of the 'progressive' or 'modern' character of the organisation. BRAC consciously projects this progressive image, insisting that women ride bicycles and motorcycles, wear the *shalwar kemise*[3] rather than the sari, and live and work together with male colleagues in offices in rural areas, away from their immediate family. These requirements press heavily upon the personal proprieties of young women in a culture which places a high value upon sheltering unmarried women. High degrees of mobility for young women, accommodation away from the family with non-kin men, all put into question their personal integrity. They are under pressure to demonstrate the organisation's progressive image, yet at the same time, preserve their 'honour', particularly if they intend eventually to marry. They are social pioneers as development agents, yet this can be at an extremely high personal cost. These contradictions account, in part, for the high drop-out rate of women staff.

BRAC has introduced policies which aim to enhance the retention of women staff, and their effectiveness as development workers, at three levels:

- adapting the organisational culture to the participation of women (changes in formal and informal behavioural norms);
- increasing their presence in the organisation and their participation in decision-making (recruiting women in greater numbers, adopting 'fast-track' promotion policies for women, providing special training in management skills);
- facilitating their physical adjustment to the demands of the workplace and their role within it (for example, making arrangements for accommodation, addressing issues of mobility, and organising essential health-care and maternity leave).

In the context of a conservative external environment, the challenge to foster genuine organisational change in women's interest is enormous. BRAC has been meeting this challenge much more directly than many other mixed-sex organisations. In 1991 its Executive Director appointed a Women's Advisory Committee to report on gender issues affecting staff, and from mid-1994, a mixed Gender Team of four BRAC staff from its Training Division, and three external consultants, has been openly raising difficult issues, pointing out, for example, contradictions between the organisation's norms of social equity and the persistence of negative attitudes towards gender equity among some staff (Rao and Kelleher, 1995:75).

The author does not intend to single out BRAC in any negative sense. On the contrary, BRAC is going further than many other mixed-gender rural development organisations (in Bangladesh and elsewhere) to solve problems faced by women staff. The following discussion highlights these problems, but they are in no way unique to BRAC. BRAC should be applauded for its openness in exposing its operations to external researchers, and for its alacrity in responding to the sensitive issues of gender-based inequalities among its staff and in their work.

The 'gendered' organisation of space

The way most rural development organisations approach the issue of physical space reflects not only men's physical capacities, but male social freedoms. Men are able to travel long distances alone, they are able to live with strangers in office accommodation without their physical integrity and security coming under threat, or their personal honour being damaged. Men are able to eat in public and relieve themselves in public without criticism. Men may also find it easier than women to establish a clear division between private space and public space, as they often do not have responsibilities for child care and for domestic work.

Living arrangements

Working in rural areas poses problems for staff, because it often means that they must move far from their homes and adjust to a new environment. Frequent transfers can exacerbate these problems. For women, however, these problems are more severe than for men, and affect single and married women differently.

BRAC has a well-developed infrastructure of rural offices which also serve as living quarters for staff. These are busy centres from which credit is dispensed, training courses are offered, where supplies are stored, and paper work is conducted. All regular staff, field workers (Programme Organisers — POs) and their office managers (Area Managers — AMs[4]), are housed in these Area Offices, with POs

sharing rooms. Only the AM has the right to have a family resident in the Area Office. The majority of POs are single; however, those who are married are generally living away from their marital families. There is a guest room for family visitors. Thus, few staff, male or female, have domestic or family responsibilities to distract from work obligations. All staff eat together, and their meals are provided by a cook, which frees staff from concerns with shopping and food preparation.

When women live with men to whom they are not related, their personal integrity is questioned and their physical security is at risk. Women and men POs live on separate sides of courtyard spaces at the back of the offices. BRAC has responded to some of the gender-related problems by elaborating a set of 'community living' behavioural norms which reiterate BRAC's egalitarianism and also respond to some of the challenges of larger numbers of women staff. One of these norms stipulates that women and men must never enter each others' rooms, and others stress the importance of respectful behaviour between women and men.

For single women, living far from home means the loss of the security and support provided by the family. Also, it becomes more difficult to begin arrangements for marriage, as families are not close enough to consult with daughters and introduce them to prospective partners.

Travel and mobility

Rural development work requires high degrees of mobility under difficult conditions. Staff must travel considerable distances each day to reach the village groups they supervise. Often they must travel on dirt roads and paths, and in the rainy season, villages can only be reached on foot, over very wet and muddy paths. In the heat of the dry season travel becomes very strenuous and exhausting. POs are supplied with a bicycle and must cycle for six months to a year, after which they ride motorcycles. Both women and men POs in BRAC travel between 11 and 17 kilometres every day. All AMs travel by motorcycle.

Bangladeshi women face problems when travelling in rural areas. In recognition of this, BRAC tries to ensure that the village groups which women staff supervise are close to the office, and clustered together, to minimise the distances which women staff travel. This can sometimes cause resentment among men, who have to travel further. Women travelling alone in rural areas is itself a new phenomenon; travelling by bicycle or motorcycle is very unconventional for women. BRAC provides gender-segregated training for staff in riding bicycles and motorcycles. It also makes sure that women gain support from the fact that other women in an operational area are also using bicycles and motorcycles.

Many of the women staff said that they faced considerable hostility from villagers because of their freedom of movement, and they also feared for their safety. As a woman AM said: 'A man can go wherever necessary, quite quickly. I don't have that kind of mobility. I feel helpless and ashamed of this. I have to make elaborate preparations for any journey: where, when, will it be dark, what kind of criticism will I face?' It is widely held within BRAC that the main reasons for the high early drop-out rate of women staff has to do with their reluctance to ride bicycles. Some women staff said that villagers, especially young men, often tried to make them fall off their bicycles by distracting them, throwing sticks into the spokes of their wheels, or chasing them. On main roads, women who ride motorcycles say that car-drivers often attempt to push them off the road and frighten them. Many women try to travel in groups with other women staff. They sometimes travel with male colleagues,

but this can arouse criticism. BRAC discourages women and men from travelling on the same motorcycle.

There are some important advantages for women in riding these vehicles. First, it has a strong public impact, and can help in changing attitudes to women's mobility. Some women in village groups expressed their admiration for BRAC women field workers because of their courage. Second, some women said they felt that travelling by motorcycle is a status symbol and can enhance the status of women field workers. And third, many women expressed a feeling of pride and accomplishment in their freedom of movement and their skill. According to one PO: 'People say that I have no parents, couldn't get educated. Young men on the roadside laugh at me. When they laugh. I stop and talk with them. And from the next day they shut up. I ride better than men — no one can ride a bike like me.'

Riding motorcycles can also provide a form of protection for women staff in the sense that the speed and noise of the vehicle can shield them from verbal and other attacks, as suggested in this quote from an AM: 'People make bad comments. They say that our country will be spoiled by women ... But on the motorbike I cannot hear the comments — because of the speed, the sound, the helmet!'

Time and gender

This service [my work] is for my life. It shouldn't be that life is for this service. Where life is a priority, one cannot do this work.
BRAC woman PO

Organisational systems for managing time affect staff in the office and the field, in terms of the pattern of the working day, and also of a life-time's career.

Managing time day-to-day
Rural development work requires activities which cannot be confined within the

normal nine-to-five office day. Village women's groups may be most accessible for development workers very early in the morning, before the working day begins; while men's groups may only be available for discussions at night, after dark. Crises in villages do not respect weekends or office hours, and can require responses from staff at unconventional times. Regular aspects of the working cycle (such as credit disbursement and recovery) are continuous throughout the year.

Having staff living in the office also means that the office, in effect, is never closed — in an emergency, staff are always on hand to make a rapid response. The working day generally starts at 6am, when POs meet with village workers — the Programme Assistants — to give instructions. Field visits to monitor groups, collect savings and loan repayments, and conduct training are done in the mornings and after lunch, and the afternoon is used for paperwork and training. For many staff, the working day does not end until 10pm.

The high work intensity in the field, and the spreading of working hours beyond normal office hours, means that women with families will lack time for domestic responsibilities, and will have to bear the costs of child care and domestic help. Some of these difficulties become apparent when examining the living arrangements of married staff. Only 25 per cent of married women POs and AMs lived with their spouses and children, compared to 50 per cent of married men.

It is difficult for women staff living at the Area Office to find time to spend with their husbands. The guest room only allows couples to stay together for very short visits. At the same time, the working culture is such that there is little spare time for visits, and also, other staff members within the compound can be disapproving of these privileges, as shown in this account from a woman PO: 'Not long after I joined, my husband came to visit me but

my colleagues were rude. They didn't talk to him, and looked at him like he was a stranger ... he felt insulted and said he wouldn't come again. He isn't happy about this job because it is so time-consuming.'

A woman AM said: 'My husband ... had no idea what BRAC work involves. Over the last five months (since the wedding) we have spent 14 days together. Over the last month he wrote to me four times and I never wrote once. In his last letter he wrote: "I think you don't need me for your life".' These problems can make it hard to adjust to the working environment, and married staff experience tension and stress because of being separated from their families: 'Married people don't get permission to stay outside of the office. This hampers work because it causes ill-will. Working against your heart.'

Life-cycle career time-management
The typical career path followed by the majority of staff in any organisation will reflect what, over time, has been the most effective way for employees to manage the relationship between their lives and their work. This means striking a balance between significant events in their lives — such as acquiring qualifications, gaining job experience, getting married, having children — and performing well in the organisation in order to move up promotional ladders. In BRAC, the typical life-cycle career path relates to the way men organise their lives and their work.

A staff member will typically join at the level of PO at the age of 27, after having completed a Master's degree. A minimum of two years' field work are expected before promotion to AM. At this point, the staff member acquires more personal space in BRAC living quarters: big enough to have a family. This is also one of the periods of the most intense activity in the field, involving considerable long-distance travel to regional offices and the head office, very long hours, and substantial responsibility. Ten years of this, and there may be a chance of promotion to the position of Regional Manager, or to head office.

For women, this life-cycle career path poses considerable difficulties. At 27, many women may already be married, and since BRAC prefers to hire single people, this may discourage them from applying for jobs. On promotion to the AM level, women will be given the space at the Area Office to accommodate a family, but they will have difficulties persuading their husband to come and live in the Area Office, as husbands are often unwilling to abandon jobs and move to follow their wives. Among married staff who had been transferred, more married women with children than men with children had to move without bringing their spouse or children with them.

If women have children, it becomes very difficult for them to manage the intense work demands which they face as field managers. Another problem is that the kind of work they do may dissuade prospective partners from marrying them at all. It is noticeable that women staff are marrying later than the average age for women of their education levels and social groups: women AMs, for instance, are marrying at around 30 years of age, and some women cite the need to get married as the reason for leaving BRAC.

Women are thus placed in an ambiguous situation. While working for BRAC may give some a much-wanted opportunity to avoid early marriage, it may make it more difficult to marry, and in a culture in which marriage is almost universal, this may encourage women to leave. This is a great loss to BRAC, postponing the development of a cadre of experienced women staff who are able to make a sustained mark upon the organisation and its work.

Child care

Child care and domestic labour tends to remain the responsibility of women even though they work full-time, and this undermines their ability to compete with men at work, and develop their own capacities. Our research showed that not one woman was able to rely on a spouse for child care, and the majority relied on a relative for this service. While most respondents felt reasonably secure about leaving their children with relatives, those who relied on servants felt uneasy about the quality of care their children were receiving. Long working days, and residence at the Area Office, mean that there is little flexibility for parents to respond to family emergencies. One woman field worker said: 'The day I joined my son was very sick. Several days later, I told the PO-in-charge that I wanted to go home to see my son but I was refused and I was told: "if you have children why did you come to do this job?" I cried, and then I left anyway to see my son.'

Over half of married BRAC women faced objections from their husbands because their work caused them to neglect their domestic obligations. While some women had husbands who adjusted to their wife's work by taking on domestic tasks, these were in a minority, and much more typical was the situation, reported by a woman field worker in a government organisation: 'When the children are sick it is me that has to stay at home. If I tell my husband that he has to do it then he says that I should just leave the job. He cannot accept it even if I am late from the office.'

All staff, of course, have the right to take leave to fulfil family responsibilities, and BRAC has introduced a special provision in recognition of women's greater family obligations — they are allowed an additional six days of leave a year. Also, AMs are encouraged to allow new women recruits leave within their first month in order to cope with homesickness and to reassure their families. The intensity of work in a rapidly expanding organisation, however, means that staff do not always take up their entitlement to leave. The nature of the working culture is such that people who do not take leave are highly regarded for their commitment and dedication. Women who take their leave may therefore be derided for lacking commitment, or resented by men who do not take as much leave. Indeed, supervisors often indicate on staff appraisal forms that staff have not taken leave: this is seen as a sign of commitment.

Health and sexuality

The organisation of space and time have an impact on the health of staff and on how they manage their sexuality. Organisational culture affects the ways the physical capabilities of men and women are valued, or alternatively, derided.

Health

The rigours of working in rural areas require stamina, and can result in health problems for both men and women. Our research showed that as many men as women are exhausted by field work. The majority of field staff of both sexes who reported problems said that their main problem was fatigue and physical strain.

Gender issues in health

For many women, physical exertion is something they are unaccustomed to. Vigorous forms of exercise are aften not considered suitable for young women in Bangladesh. Our research showed there is a sharp difference between women and men staff in terms of their history of physical exercise, with almost all the men having played sports. Ironically, the women whose jobs involve the greatest amount of physical exertion (the village-level workers) had the least exposure to

sports in their youth. Women higher up in the hierarchy have had more exposure to physical exercise. Involvement in sport is correlated with place of origin and class status: staff from urban and higher-class backgrounds tend to have played more sports than staff from rural backgrounds.

Women experience particular health problems caused by the absence of certain basic facilities in the rural environment. For example, there are few eating facilities in the field which are appropriate for women, who often do not feel comfortable eating in public restaurants. Women often skip meals, which contributes to gastric problems and feelings of exhaustion.

There are no sanitation facilities in the field for women, and modesty prohibits them from using bushes in the way men can. Women staff said they would avoid drinking water during the day because of this. Insufficient water in a hot and exhausting working environment can result in dehydration, and can exacerbate urinary tract infections, and difficulties managing menstruation. BRAC proposed, at the time of this study, to make sure that proper latrines were built in every village where women worked. Unfortunately, the resentment which men express about the special measures sometimes needed to accommodate women's bodily needs suggests that these needs are treated as constraints on the organisation, rather than simply a necessary feature of working with women.

Reproductive health issues

Women also experience problems related to their reproductive health. BRAC gives three months' maternity leave to women staff, which is generous by local standards. About half of the women in the sample who had children had trouble adjusting once they returned to work, in particular because there are no breast-feeding facilities in field or head offices, and it was difficult for them to arrange for satisfactory milk substitutes for their babies. In some cases, this resulted in health problems for mother and infant. As with most organisations in Bangladesh and elsewhere, there was no paternity leave for men in BRAC, and some men said that requests for short periods of leave when their children were born were refused.

Menstruation raises a set of problems in a work environment with inadequate facilities both in the field and office. Where work requires physical activity such as bicycling, menstruation can be a problem because of the discomfort and pain which some women experience. BRAC has an innovative policy of allowing an optional two days of 'desk leave' for women staff every month (although at the time of this study, this policy did not extend to women PAs). The desk-leave policy represents an important form of organisational adjustment to accommodate women's physical needs. Unfortunately, taking desk leave sends out a signal that one is menstruating, and women feel ashamed of making other colleagues aware of this fact. As a result, many women do not take advantage of this facility. Almost one-third of women POs felt too ashamed to ask for desk leave even when they needed it. Some said that they only felt comfortable asking for leave if their boss was a woman. Many women avoided desk leave because they did not want men to feel that women were not working as hard as them.

The prudishness about menstruation, which is seen as a symbol of women's impurity, means that neither women nor men wish to draw attention to it. This is particularly difficult for men. One male AM said: 'There is no written rule about menstruation but women would tell me they were sick and I'd say, "OK, don't go to the field", and it was implicit that it was menstruation. To be honest, I have never uttered this word from my mouth, and this is the first time I have ever spoken directly to a woman about it.' Reactions to the desk-leave policy illustrate how a special measure to recognise biological difference can be experienced instead as signalling a form of disability for women.

Sexuality

There is considerable informal surveillance of the movements of women and men staff in Area Offices, which is a reflection of the organisation's concern to maintain moral propriety in light of the fact that so many unmarried women and men are living together, unchaperoned by family. All staff must sign a 'movement register' when they leave the office during their free time, for example at weekends, to indicate their plans. This is a security measure which is important in an environment where some women development agents are the target of abuse and attack. However, it is resented by women staff, who claim that their male colleagues are not as strictly controlled in their movements as they are.

BRAC's policy on personal relationships demonstrates problems in managing sexuality within an organisation. BRAC, quite rightly, is deeply concerned to discourage sexual harassment, which is probably the most severe constraint on women's capacity to work effectively and to develop credible leadership capacities. It is hard to strike an effective balance between excessive surveillance on the one hand, and indifference on the other. It must be noted that women staff in BRAC reported a much lower incidence of sexual harassment — almost none — compared to women in the government organisation studied. However, women in BRAC felt that the organisation's concerns over sexual propriety were expressed through constraints on their behaviour, rather than on that of their male colleagues. This illustrates gender bias in patterns of managing sexuality within the organisation.

Conclusions

Is it possible or desirable to separate the public and the private? The evidence above suggests that it has been difficult for women in BRAC to be accommodated within the 'male' space of the office, or to feel at home in rural areas. Feminists have claimed that most space outside of the domestic arena, particularly the work space, is structured to favour men. They argue, therefore, for an abolition of the separation between the public and the private. That domestic space is a necessary support to public space is often denied by men, who insist on a clear demarcation between the two, yet could not even manage to turn up for work properly fed and clothed without support from the domestic arena. Feminists propose instead to acknowledge the importance of the private in the public sphere, to make it easier for women to participate in public spaces. Child-care facilities at work would be one way of doing this.

How far is it possible or even desirable to eliminate the public/private distinction at work? There are limits to how far an organisation can go in trying to compensate for the constraints imposed on women by patriarchy in the private sphere. For instance, in the case above where women's husbands persist in refusing to share child care and domestic labour responsibilities, how much can BRAC be expected to do to help women deal with this problem?

BRAC's approach to organising its field operations has been precisely towards abolishing the distinction between home and office. By providing living space for staff in the office, and communal eating facilities, some of the labour constraints of maintaining a private household are lifted for women. But instead of bringing the home to the office, by domesticating the official environment, BRAC has brought the office to the home. It has eliminated space and time for family interactions, and

for leisure, for staff. The result has been a very efficient means of monopolising their labour. This has had particularly difficult implications for women, who are much less able than men to live as though the private sphere did not exist.

The issues raised regarding marriage and family life pose a dilemma. On the one hand, the lack of time and space in BRAC field offices for people's personal lives imposes great tensions on both married and single women. Married women face acute problems in juggling their dual public and private obligations. Single women are stigmatised because of the nature of the work that they do, and are considered to be unmarriageable. Many male staff also suffer because they cannot have full family lives, and many staff object to the constraints on the ways they can interact with each other.

On the other hand, BRAC's innovative arrangements for bringing men and women together in the field are a model of a new form of gender relations in rural areas. In the conservative environment in which BRAC operates, it is important to provide young women with assurances that their honour will be protected, and to reassure rural people that BRAC is a morally upright organisation. BRAC is making it possible for young career women to postpone marriage and demonstrate to rural people a non-traditional role for women. This can have a powerful impact in terms of providing role models for others, as one interviewee pointed out: 'My colleagues say I should get married and they say the job is too hard for women to do. I object. If I do the job well, then later more women can come forward.'

Women staff have adapted BRAC's organisational image-management rules to their own needs. Some of them manage the accommodation between traditional Bangladeshi womanhood and the social pioneering aspects of their work by trying to underplay or even deny the

implications and opportunities for autonomy which their employment gives them.
However, it is a lonely process to have to
represent an organisation's progressive
image. Challenging social conventions
regarding gender inevitably causes
conflict, and makes women vulnerable to
attack, even from male colleagues who do
not necessarily believe in the progressive
ideas they are supposed to promote.

It is clear that the way women staff
have adapted their role in upholding
BRAC's image indicates some ambivalence in their feelings about their role as
social pioneers. Not only does the amount
of criticism women face because of their
unconventional appearance and behaviour bring a great deal of personal strain,
but their single status, the clothing they
are expected to wear, and the vehicles
they have to use, all pose challenges not
only to norms of decency, but to their
ability to carry out their work, as they risk
derision in the rural environment.

The constraints within which BRAC
operates — such as a conservative external
culture — seem so fixed that it is difficult to
imagine that things could be managed
differently. The important practical
question is: how far should and can management practices be changed to accommodate these problems? How far should
an organisation take responsibility for the
constraints on women's capacities which
are posed by their domestic lives and their
reproductive responsibilities?

There are very few formal employment
environments which have developed
effective responses to these problems.
Regarding women's reproductive role as
carers and marital partners, it can be
expensive for an organisation to provide
child care for staff; it is very difficult to
coordinate job transfers for two people as
co-habitees. Secondly, there are a whole set
of issues concerning positive action to
promote female participation in the work
place. How far is special provision for

women justifiable, and how far will it
provoke resentment from men? Moreover,
would such special provision undermine
the principles of merit and dedication on
which the organisation is based?

While it is not possible to answer all of
these questions, there are examples of
alternative ways of managing women in
organisations, in Bangladesh. Women's
organisations involved in rural development have taken different approaches, for
example, to reconciling the conflicting
demands of home and work, or to managing women's public work identities. They
have found ways of accommodating child
care within the office space, and of allowing women to manage their own public
identities in ways they are comfortable
with. They have supported these measures with training in women's rights and
with support for women's perspectives on
gender issues in their work.[5]

While a full discussion of women's
organisations cannot be developed here,
such organisations, despite their own
problems, and differences in size and
scope from organisations like BRAC, do
offer some possibilities for managing
women staff which mixed organisations
could consider. The stress on allowing
women to be near their own families, the
domesticating of the official environment,
respect for and non-interference in
women's personal lives, and the more
flexible use of time could all be adapted to
the working conditions of mixed organisations.

This article has tried to illustrate how
some of the practical aspects of an organisation's structure in space and time can
be 'gendered', and how this can affect
women's capacities to flourish within an
organisation. There is pressure on women
to emulate male work patterns and to
identify with the dominant culture. One
consequence can be that women staff are
less confident in developing and acting
upon their own perspectives on women's

interests in development. The ultimate test of an organisation's effectiveness in integrating women staff and in modelling new versions of gender relations in the rural areas should be whether women staff can say that their participation in the organisation has helped them to feel valued, and also, has allowed them to pursue their own visions of change in gender relations.

References

Goetz, A M (1996) 'Dis/organising gender: women development agents in state and NGO poverty-reduction programmes in Bangladesh', in Rai, S and Lievesley, G (eds) *Women and the State: International Perspectives*, Taylor and Francis, London.

Howes, M (1996) 'NGOs and the development of membership organisations: the case of Shaptagram', mimeo, IDS, Sussex.

Rao, A and Kelleher, D (1995) 'Engendering organisational change: the BRAC case', *IDS Bulletin*, 26, 3, July, Sussex.

Yasmin, T (1997) 'What is different about women's organisations?', in Goetz, A M (ed) *Breaking In, Speaking Out: Getting Institutions Right for Women in Development*, Zed Press, forthcoming.

Notes

1 This article is composed of extracts from a draft chapter for a book on the work of lower-level field-workers implementing gender and development policies in rural credit organisations in Bangladesh. It is based upon 121 in-depth interviews with field workers of two development organisations in Bangladesh, BRAC and the 'Rural Development-12' programme of the government's Bangladesh Rural Development Board. I thank BRAC for its generosity and openness in allowing me to research its operations, and I also thank the government's Rural Development — 12 programme. I am grateful to Rina Sen Gupta, my research partner, with whom the fieldwork was conducted between February and October 1993. This article concentrates on the interviews with BRAC staff.

2 In another paper (Goetz 1996) I investigate the impact of organisational cultures on women's capacity to develop a capacity for leadership in women's interests in development.

3 The *shalwar kemise* is a form of dress which is worn in urban areas by women of all ages. In rural areas, however, it is usually not worn by married women or women over the age of 16. It is a loose long shirt worn over baggy trousers.

4 There is another category of field staff: the Programme Assistants, who are village-level development workers who are not part of the professional staff structure of BRAC. Space constraints here prohibit a full discussion of the gender issues affecting this level of staff.

5 See Yasmin 1997 and Howes 1996 for a discussion of these features of management in Shaptagram Nari Swanivar Parishad (Seven Villages Women's Self-Reliance Organisation).

Implementing a Gender Policy in ACORD:

strategies, constraints, and challenges

Angela Hadjipateras

This short article examines the evolution of ACORD's approach to gender issues, and summarises the main conclusions emerging from a recent review of the organisation's gender policy. Some strengths and weaknesses of particular strategies adopted at various levels of the organisation are indicated. The article goes on to discuss future directions for the implementation.

ACORD is a consortium of 11 non-governmental organisations from Europe, Asia, and North America devoted to community-based and gender-sensitive poverty alleviation in Africa. ACORD was founded in 1976. It currently employs 550 staff, most of whom originate from, and work in, 16 countries in Africa, with a Secretariat of 29 in London. Nearly half ACORD's funding comes from the member organisations, and the rest is fairly evenly split between private, bilateral, and multilateral funding institutions.

ACORD formally established a gender policy in 1990, and initiated a review process four years later. The review was intended to document and draw lessons from the organisation's experiences of implementing the policy, both in its work with partners in Africa, and in ACORD's London-based Secretariat. A consultant was commissioned to undertake the research in the field. This was carried out during 1994-6 and included a survey of field programmes. In 1996, another gender consultant was commissioned to carry out a case study of the institution as a whole.[1]

Evolution of the policy

ACORD first began considering the place of women in its work in the mid-1980s, as the UN Decade for Women (1975-85) was drawing to a close. In January 1988, a policy statement on 'working with women' was drawn up in consultation with field and Secretariat staff, and in April that year a Women in Development (WID) Programme Policy was approved by the Assembly, the ultimate decision-making body within ACORD.

This policy stressed the need to enhance women's access to resources, and their participation in activities and decision-making processes, at all levels of the organisation's programme work in Africa. These goals were to be promoted by a programme of activities, including the creation of Women's Officer posts, and the establishment of budget lines to fund training, networking and inter-programme exchanges.

After the first year, a review noted that, while some progress had been made, this had fallen short of expectations. Factors hindering progress were identified as lack of interest by major donors, and some 'dragging of feet' by staff — mainly field staff but also some senior managers.

Discussion of the review led to the decision to introduce a gender policy which, in line with wider development theory and practice, takes culturally-determined gender relations as the focus of analysis and promotes the reduction, if not elimination, of gender-based inequities in the communities where ACORD works. This new approach would facilitate a better understanding of women's position within different cultural contexts. However, the change in policy caused some confusion at the field level, and some staff felt the policy was being introduced in a top-down manner.

ACORD's gender policy was promoted primarily through an extensive programme of training. In addition, a full-time Gender Officer post was created in London, to provide advice and support to programmes in the field and to promote gender awareness within the Secretariat. In order to monitor progress, programmes were required to report on the implementation of the policy in their annual reports.

The impact on communities and individuals

One of the aims of the 1990 review process was to assess if, and how, the organisational gender policy had affected the design and implementation of ACORD's programme interventions, and, by extension, the lives of, and relationships between, the men and women of the communities with which ACORD works.

The analytical framework adopted for the research was one developed by Sara Hlupekile Longwe, which identifies five distinct steps along the path towards equality between men and women. These five steps are improvements for women in terms of: *welfare* (basic survival), *access to resources* (including opportunities for self-realisation); *conscientisation* (an awareness of and will to alter gender inequalities); *participation* (including an equal role in decision-making); and *control* (in both the personal and public domains).

The research concluded that the greatest gains for women overall, throughout ACORD's programmes, have been in the spheres of welfare, access to resources, conscientisation, and, to a lesser extent, participation. One example is of women participating in a credit programme in Port Sudan, who have overcome the cultural barriers constraining women's role in commerce: the programme provides credit to roughly equal numbers of men and women. A second example of increased participation comes from ACORD's programme in Luanda, Angola, where there are now more women on Water Committees and other community management structures. Lastly, the Gulu programme in Uganda has enhanced women's welfare and status, through promoting their participation in productive loan schemes alongside men.

However, ACORD's programmes appear to have had limited impact in terms of the ultimate 'level' of the Longwe framework: control. Even here, there have been a few breakthroughs, such as in Gao, Mali, where ACORD has been instrumental in enabling some women to increase their control over rice production (a critical economic resource in the region), and in Gulu, Uganda, where AIDS training has helped some women make more informed choices in terms of sexual practices. But such examples are few and far between; overall, little progress appears to have been made in shifting the prevailing imbalance of power and control in relations between men and women.

Successful strategies and methodologies

The research identified a number of strategies that appear to have promoted positive outcomes for women. These fall into two broad categories: *programming* and *organisational* strategies.

Programming strategies

Gender-awareness training: The research suggested that raising awareness of gender issues among both men and women, using tools of gender analysis such as the Harvard framework,[2] is perhaps the single most effective means of improving and potentially transforming gender relations. For example, in Gulu, Uganda, ACORD provided training for a pool of community-based trainers, to disseminate awareness of power relations between women and men, in ways which were relevant to the particular context.

At one gender-training session in Gulu, men and women were asked to form separate groups, and to produce a daily work record. The women's record of activities showed that they worked from dawn to dusk without a break, whereas the men's showed that they had ample leisure-time. When the two groups came together to discuss and compare their respective work-patterns, the fact that women worked roughly twice as many hours as men became the subject of a lively debate. Following this discussion, the whole group resolved to invest in buying grinding mills and hoes, in order to facilitate women's work in grinding and weeding which took up the greatest part of their time.

Working with mixed groups: The research found that working with mixed groups

further consolidated the impact of gender-awareness training, by enhancing mutual understanding, respect, and co-operation. For example, an all-male production group in Mali agreed, as a result of some pressure from ACORD, to accept women members. While this agreement had initially been somewhat reluctant, during a meeting held as part of the gender research, the men stated that the women's contribution had become essential. However, to have an acknowledged role in production is not the same as gaining control. An important factor in gaining control is confidence on the part of women, as stated below.

Working with women-only groups: The research findings indicated that women may also need to meet separately. In one of ACORD's programmes in Lubango, Angola, women have recently formed a group to discuss a variety of issues. The women report that this has helped them to build up their confidence, and overcome their fear of expressing their views in public. As a result, many of the women now participate more actively in other community groups, such as the local Health Commission. The women also said that the programme has built up solidarity and friendship between the women in the community, many of whom had previously felt very isolated.

Promotion of female leadership: A common strategy adopted by many ACORD programmes is to require all mixed groups to appoint one male and one female representative. Women are also encouraged to take on management responsibilities. Besides enhancing their own confidence and status, both in the wider community and at home, successful women leaders serve as role-models for other women. In ACORD's programme in Chad, one of the literacy trainers is a woman, and one of the classes she taught included her husband! This caused quite a stir in the community, and her example is frequently used as proof of women's abilities.

Gender-aware participatory planning and evaluation: Many ACORD programmes have instituted participatory planning and evaluation processes using methods, such as PRA[3] to promote community participation. However, the use of participatory methods does not in itself ensure that women's views and priorities are necessarily represented; the methods must be gender-sensitive.

In Gulu, groups meet annually to discuss their work and plan the following year's activities. However, the first such meeting coincided with the busiest time of the year for women, so very few women came, and those that did attend sat at the back of the room and hardly spoke. The following year, the issues of timing and of promoting full participation were both addressed. The meeting was held at a more convenient time, and seats were arranged in a circle. The result was a significant improvement in the levels of attendance and participation of women.

Organisational strategies

Gender-awareness training: The staff of an organisation must also receive training. Awareness of gender issues is essential for an understanding of, and commitment to, gender equity. In ACORD's London Secretariat, gender training helped to reveal subtle forms of gender discrimination operating within the office.

In addition, training was found to be most effective when closely linked to programme activities. In Mali, staff who participated in a regional gender workshop claimed that this marked a turning-point in the programme's approach; previously, women's activities were completely marginalised, whereas after the workshop staff were at least attempting (though with limited success)

to integrate women fully into the programme's main activities. However, the research findings suggested that unless gender training for staff is regularly updated, and includes all staff, not only gender specialists, its impact is limited.

Spreading responsibility for gender: The research showed that the degree to which gender awareness is integrated into all spheres of programme activity is related to where responsibility lies for implementing the gender policy. The most effective staff structure was found in Gulu, where a Gender Committee consists of a cross-section of staff, who are collectively responsible for developing a strategy in line with the policy. A Gender Officer coordinates this work.

Recruitment and promotion of women staff: The research findings confirm that there is a clear link between ensuring that gender concerns are fully integrated in ACORD's programme, and the gender balance of ACORD's staff. Not only is a 'critical mass' of women staff important in ensuring that gender concerns are not marginalised, but potential charges of hypocrisy can be avoided if ACORD practises what it preaches! In addition, employing female staff members is essential in order to gain access to women in some communities.

While the number of women on the staff as a whole is critical, female participation, and representation, at senior management levels is also critical, as is the commitment of all senior management to gender equity. In ACORD, some of the most ground-breaking programmes in gender terms are those managed by female staff with a strong commitment to gender equity.[4]

Networks for women staff: ACORD's women staff welcome opportunities to meet to discuss issues and dilemmas relating to their own lives, as well as issues related to the programme. They claim that such networking can help to increase gender-awareness in programming. However, such networks have not always proved beneficial; male staff have sometimes resented their exclusion.

Direct field involvement in research: The research process itself has proved to be effective in implementing the gender policy, in a number of ways. Direct involvement of staff in the planning and carrying out of the research has enhanced their commitment to working on gender issues. Staff have been provided with an opportunity to analyse their work, consolidate their knowledge, and try out new methods. Lastly, the overall positive response of the communities themselves to work on gender issues has confirmed the value and relevance of this work.

Organisational weaknesses

The research, including the institutional case study, explored factors, both internal and external, which weaken or subvert the implementation of the gender policy. These are some of the points identified:

Different understandings of the policy
A lack of clarity as to the aims and objectives of gender work hampers the organisation's ability to develop effective strategies and appropriate indicators for monitoring progress. Whereas most staff within ACORD are aware of the existence of the policy, few are familiar with its content. There are wide variations in the way the policy is understood; for some, 'gender' is synonymous with 'women', and is seen either as concerned with setting up activities specifically directed at women (usually ones that reinforce women's traditional roles) or as a way of surreptitiously promoting Western-inspired feminist goals. For others, the policy provides a justification for moving away from a WID concept to work more closely with men as well. As one male staff-member noted: 'I am much happier

with ACORD's new gender policy as our women do not need to be "liberated", and besides, it is not fair that men should be left out.'

Cultural resistance
To a great extent, the above-mentioned difficulties are a reflection of the inevitable conflict of interests which arises when gender imbalances are addressed. While most staff express support, discussions held as part of the research revealed fears about and, in some cases, outright hostility to the gender policy, on the part of both staff and community members.

Confusion as to responsibility and procedure
It is unclear who, at ACORD's Secretariat, is ultimately responsible for ensuring that the policy is implemented. The Gender Officer is part of the Research and Policy Programme (RAPP), which is separate from the Programme Department (PD). RAPP's role is mainly an advisory one, whereas the PD is responsible for the overall implementation of programmes, including their gender dimension. Within ACORD's international offices, even where Gender Officers exist, their status and authority tends to be limited.

These difficulties are compounded by the fact that the policy takes the form of a statement of goals and principles, but does not provide any clear guidelines for their implementation in practice.

Weak accountability mechanisms
The main tool for making ACORD programmes and staff accountable for their programme work, including that on gender, is the annual report.[5] However, the standard of reporting is very uneven, and there have been few attempts to remedy this. Staff also complain that they get no feedback from the Secretariat. This lack of support undermines the usefulness of the annual report as a mechanism for monitoring and improving programmes.

Programmes are reviewed individually, and standards may differ from one programme to another. The nature of gender work itself, including the fact that it takes place in widely varying cultural and socio-economic contexts, makes it virtually impossible to devise a set of uniform criteria for assessing programme performance in gender terms. Accountability is weakened by the absence of agreed minimum standards.

Lack of 'gender impact indicators'

The lack of performance indicators is a weakness in ACORD programmes and one that the organisation has been trying to address over the last two years. In the case of gender, this problem is accentuated by the lack of clarity about objectives. Many programmes still equate gender work with equal participation of women, and simply collect figures on beneficiaries broken down by sex. A few also include some qualitative information, including case studies or anecdotes, indicating impact on gender relations, or changes in women's status.

The fact that there is no systematic recording of the perceived 'impact' of ACORD's work on gender issues reflects both the difficulty of determining indicators of impact for social development work, and the fact that gender trainers and practitioners have only recently begun to address this difficulty. In the face of increasing funding pressures and donor concerns with efficiency, programmes need to be able to demonstrate impact in tangible terms.

Training inadequacies

Despite the intensification of training following the introduction of the gender policy, weaknesses still exist. In particular, there is little in the way of follow-up or guided supervision to help staff to consolidate their understanding and apply the tools of gender analysis. Another problem is that, owing to the irregularity of the training and high staff turnover rates, at any given time a significant proportion of staff are likely not to have received even basic gender-awareness training. This applies to the Secretariat as well as field staff.[6]

Under-representation of women staff

ACORD has an equal opportunities policy, which has helped to achieve gender balance among field staff, as well as Regional Programme Officers in the Secretariat. However, at the programme level, a survey carried out as part of the gender research[7] revealed that women staff are still under-represented overall and particularly at management levels. Some programmes have taken proactive measures, such as generous parental leave provisions and the adoption of a positive discrimination policy for recruitment, promotion, and training. However, the pressures and demands of most field posts present obstacles to staff with family responsibilities. In addition, despite attempts to do so, it has not been possible to improve the 2:1 ratio of male to female staff at the senior management level.

Inadequate resources

Most of the above problems are compounded by the lack of resources for the promotion of gender work. While there is some donor interest in supporting gender initiatives, it is difficult to get funding for non-programme-specific costs, such as additional staff recruitment, staff training, research, networking and dissemination. This has affected the pace of progress, particularly with respect to programme training needs.

Lessons and challenges for the future

ACORD's experience shows that to bring about tangible changes in terms of gender equity in the organisation and the communities with which it works, a multipronged strategy is required. Every aspect of organisational functioning, from management structures to methods used in work with communities, must be addressed.

One valuable lesson that can be learned from ACORD's experience is the importance of being able to look self-critically at one's own organisation. As a result of the gender review process, work on gender issues has become central in ACORD's current five-year strategic plan. This plan commits the organisation to revising the existing gender policy, in consultation with all field programmes, and striving for equality for men and women in programme outcomes, and equal numbers of male and female staff throughout the organisation. In addition, a comprehensive plan for 'centralising gender' over the next five years, produced by the Gender Officer, has been discussed by the Secretariat. It remains to be seen whether the commitment and resources for implementing this plan will be found, but it seems likely that they will be forthcoming.

Angela Hadjipateras is Gender Officer in the Research and Policy Programme of ACORD. She can be contacted at ACORD, Francis House, Francis Street, London SW1P 1DQ, UK. Tel: 0171 828 7611/7612; fax: 0171 976 6113; e-mail: acord@gn.org.apc

Notes

1 The first consultant was Angela Hadjipateras, and the second, Bridget Byrne. The five studies were carried out during 1995/6 by a consultant attached to ACORD's Research and Policy Programme (RAPP) in Mali (Gao), Uganda (Gulu), Ethiopia (Dire Dawa), Angola (Luanda and Lubango) and Sudan (Port Sudan). ACORD field staff were directly involved in the analysis of their work and in the planning and organisation of visits to community groups. The Case Study by an external consultant, Bridget Byrne, was completed in September 1996.

2 The Harvard framework is used for highlighting differences in gender roles, as well as gender-based differences in terms of access to and control over resources.

3 Participatory Rural Appraisal (PRA) is a set of tools aimed at maximising the level of participation of all community members in project planning. It can also be used for evaluation purposes and has been applied in urban, as well as rural settings.

4 For example, the Dire Dawa programme in Ethiopia and a number of programmes in Rwanda.

5 The Annual Report is written by programme field staff and is used as a management tool by the Secretariat, as well as being sent out to programme funders.

6 ACORD is currently developing a modular training programme using a thematic approach which is aimed at enabling staff to apply gender analysis to all areas of their work, from setting up credit groups to planning latrine construction or planting of trees. Once it is up and running, this training package will enable training to be regularly updated and facilitate the full integration of gender analysis in the day-to-day work of programmes.

7 The survey covered 16 out of a total of 35 programmes.

Establishing a feminist culture:

the experience of Zimbabwe Women's Resource Centre and Network

Hope Chigudu

This is an account of the experience of ZWRCN in attempting to establish a feminist organisational culture, analysing the successes, and describing the pitfalls encountered. In order to create such an organisational culture, a shared vision is essential. The author raises critical issues for organisations wishing to question the ways of working of traditional bureaucracies. How can a culture based on feminist principles maintain a sense of professionalism, both within and outside the organisation?

In 1988, I and a colleague at Zimbabwe's Ministry of Community Development and Women's Affairs began discussing the problem of a lack of a central place where information on women and development, and literature on feminism, could be made available. We agreed that what was needed was a women's resource centre. By 1990, together with other women in the country, we had raised initial funds from the Global Fund for Women (subsequent funding has come from multilateral and bilateral donors), and rented a small office. This was the start of the Zimbabwe Women's Resource Centre and Network (ZWRCN).

Today, ZWRCN has built up a collection of 4,000 documents relating to gender and feminist issues, in Zimbabwe and the region; in addition, the organisation operates a rural libraries programme. Our objectives are:

- to promote and strengthen inter-organisational networking activities for the exchange of experience and information on gender and development issues;

- to promote greater gender awareness through the collection and dissemination of information on gender and development issues;

- to promote among relevant agencies, the adoption of gender-sensitive information systems so that their programmes are amenable to gender analysis;

- to repackage information, where desirable and possible, so that it can more easily be disseminated to users;

- to improve the availability of information to rural women;

- to provide gender information to inform the policy and planning processes of relevant government ministries and NGOs;

- to help to fill information gaps through research projects.

The strategy of the ZWRCN is to focus at both community and 'policy-making' level (although policies are formed throughout society, from the household upwards). In this way we aim to play a part in bringing about critical changes in the decisions which affect women's lives.

Rejecting a 'masculine' organisational culture

An organisational culture helps to create standards of what is acceptable or not acceptable. From the beginning, the founder members of the ZWRCN wanted to avoid a mainstream organisational culture,[1] and instead establish a feminist culture for our organisation. Our argument was that mainstream management models are patriarchal in nature, and eliminate respect for individuals, flexibility, and differences. In comparison, a 'feminist' culture can be characterised as challenging the idea of patriarchal control (where the head of the family defines everybody's needs). By questioning what is perceived by many to be a given, our vision of a feminist culture is of one which fosters liberty, self-determination, personal dignity, and a higher quality of life.

Challenging patriarchal structures within ZWRCN

Organisational culture has an internal, as well as an external, dimension. Our reasoning was that if ZWRCN was to bring about change in society, that change had to start from within. Therefore, it is pertinent to examine the way people treat each other within the organisation, as well as how they treat their constituents and contacts in the outside world.

Just as we wanted to be free of domination by men, we also wanted a culture for ZWRCN which freed women from domination by other women. We felt that a feminist organisational culture would be one where every person would feel needed and respected, with their talents used and recognised. It should be a culture based on the values of sisterhood, openness, democracy, and team-work. However, the issues of status and practical conditions of employment for staff would have to be addressed.

We wanted an empowered staff, equipped with knowledge, awareness, and skills. We wanted a participatory type of leadership. We wanted a management style that would enable staff to question and criticise, but also feel confident in offering alternatives. We envisaged that such a culture would enable them to question their own condition and position, both within the organisation and within the wider society. We wanted a supportive culture. We were confident that we could transform the structures and institutions that perpetuate social inequality and create an organisation in which everyone is striving for the same objectives. We were ready to change the world!

It was with this understanding of a feminist culture in mind that we set out to build ZWRCN.

Setting up a new structure

A Board of Trustees is a legal requirement for all Zimbabwean organisations. Three of the founder members, together with two other people, constituted the Board. We created posts, including that of Director, but hoped that this position would rotate among members of staff, as would most of the other posts. On the first day of ZWRCN's existence, we had two staff members, and the rest of us worked as volunteers.

Our organisational structure reflected our commitment to minimal hierarchy. We hoped that such a structure would facilitate the creation of a team spirit, a sense of mission, passion, purpose, excitement, and innovation. We were rejecting not only the principle of a hierarchical organisation, but the complex, bureaucratic ways of working which tend to accompany this.

We hoped that the structure of ZWRCN would develop along the lines of a family without a household head, where family members contribute their different knowledge, skills, and resources. The family may have disagreements and debates, but essentially the structure is 'flat'.

Capacity-building and staff development

We were aware that a feminist culture would not evolve automatically. Since it challenges previously unquestioned patriarchal structures (Joseph 1996), a commitment to building a feminist organisation involves helping staff to acquire new knowledge and skills, and a different understanding of how to manage organisations.

The organisation needed a Director and staff who were risk-takers, (the culture we were adopting was risky) prepared to take on controversial issues, and who were sensitive to feminism, and not afraid of the word. But most of the 15 new staff we have recruited since ZWRCN's inception are ambivalent about being identified as feminists. They are familiar with the bureaucratic structures of government and most NGOs in Zimbabwe, where professional success is both a function and expression of a person's ability to conform to convention. They were familiar with the bureaucratic modes of behaviour, procedures, dress, and management styles.

We needed to overcome the paradox of attempting to build an organisation on a vision, which was not yet fully shared; until then it would be hard for us, as founder members, to relinquish control, and delegate responsibility, to women who did not consider themselves to be feminists.

Gender training

When ZWRCN was set up, very few Zimbabwean professionals had had the opportunity to undergo gender training sessions, or exposure to consciousness-raising. Our first step was to start Gender and Development (GAD) talks, held once a week during the lunch-break. The aim of the talks was two-fold: first, to ground ourselves in a shared understanding of feminist theory; second, to demystify our view of organisational culture, enabling all staff members to share in the founder members' vision. However, as time went on, and members of the public wanted to attend the GAD talks, the talks lost their original significance.

Mentoring and role-models

Most women's organisations value feminism, but reward patriarchy in the workplace. Before we are able to make a complete change, we need new mentors and models. We tried to build staff capacity by ensuring that the relationship between Board Members (most of whom were founder members) and staff was collegial, and mutually supportive. The Board Members devised a strategy for passing on their knowledge and expertise to the young programme staff. Each staff member was 'apprenticed' to a member of the Board. We tried to match the activities of the organisation with the skills and areas of expertise of Board Members, who would be responsible for mentoring, and facilitating each staff member's growth towards autonomy and independence.

However, though the decision to try this way of working was discussed with the then Director, it was not long before she felt undermined by the close working relationships which developed. She complained to the Board that by working directly with staff, Board Members were usurping her power. Already, at this early stage in the evolution of the organisation, we had begun to realise the difficulties of establishing a feminist culture, and the dilemmas which could arise over the concepts of *power* and *control*.

Fostering a non-hierarchical culture

Issues of power kept creeping into our debates. Is pursuing a goal in line with the organisation's vision more important than observing organisational procedure? For example, can — or should — activists be tied down to job descriptions? If a contentious issue needs to be resolved immediately, should it really matter whose job description it falls under? What happens if there is no time to go through the chain of command, before taking action?

One example of our attempt to foster non-hierarchical ways of working was the agreement that members of staff would be represented on the selection panels for recruitment of senior members of staff, including the Director. We felt that staff have a valid opinion on whether or not a candidate would be able to lead them.

In an effort to reject patriarchal attitudes and dominating ways of interacting with colleagues, we tried very hard to create an environment in which junior members of staff could express themselves as freely as anybody else. Openness about all aspects of the work of the organisation was encouraged; for example, in the early days, all staff members were allowed to attend Board meetings, most of which were held in a friendly atmosphere in our homes. However, by 1993, as the Board expanded, bureaucratic ways of working seemed to take over, and staff members stopped attending Board meetings.

Dress codes

Our debates over dress codes exemplify the issue of how far one can run an organisation on an assumption of shared values. For women, clothing is a significant matter on two counts; first, in wider society, there is an accepted dress code of modesty; ostensibly 'Westernised' items of dress may offend men as they see women challenging the 'traditional' values of their communities. Secondly, women in male-dominated offices are already challenging norms by their mere presence; and the option of conventional 'business' dressing — the male suit — is not open to them. Conservative, smart dressing is the key to acceptability.

The time came when several staff members started coming to work wearing cowboy hats. We did not know whether to intervene or not, since we did not have a formal code of dress; within feminist culture, were we supposed to have one? To most of us, it did not matter very much how one dressed, as long as one carried out one's work; and yet eyebrows were raised by colleagues in other organisations — not only government bureaucracies, but other women's organisations — and the wider public.

A conservative dress-code gives credibility to women in our society, as in most throughout the world; hence, more credibility to the organisation. Here we were once again torn between 'traditional' demands that women conform to the norms of society and mainstream organisational practice, and the feminist ideal that a woman should be free to express her individuality in whatever way she wishes.

Organisational expansion and alternative cultures

As the organisation expanded and new people joined, they came with their own expectations, and it was difficult to keep up the same momentum for politicisation as we had done in the early years. ZWRCN evolved to include women who regarded themselves as 'professionals' in a bureaucratic sense, and others whom the first group regarded (and described openly) as 'over-empowered' women.

It was difficult for long-serving members of staff to work with new bureaucratically-minded managers who expected to have tea made for them – and on time! – and who did not expect a junior officer to answer back. These managers wanted to be accorded the respect due to the head of the family. I remember one Director insisting that if the Board did not dismiss one 'over-empowered officer', she would resign. In my capacity as a founder member and Vice-Chairperson of the organisation, I felt I had to see the 'junior' officer concerned to explain that she had to learn to do what her boss wanted. For me this was painful, but what choice did I have? I did not want her to lose her job. I had known this member of staff for a long time, and understood that the clash was a stage in her own journey towards feeling empowered.

Again, in describing this situation I feel drawn to making a comparison between working relationships and relationships within the family: I had to caution the junior officer like a mother telling a daughter who complains about a husband that 'men are like that, just keep quiet and obey if you want to save the marriage'!

Modes of address

Other, apparently minor, issues signalled the ways in which the organisational culture was changing. One such issue was the question of how we should address each other. At the inception of the organisation, some of us made it clear that we wanted to be addressed by our first names; however, this was not a unanimous decision. Others insisted on titles: one woman with a doctorate asked us to call her Dr. (Mrs) X. We were uncomfortable; we explained to her, in a friendly manner, that the organisation was promoting a culture of modesty, and that we were on first-name terms. We were using this

informal mode of address as we believed it to be non-hierarchical, and thereby consistent with the values of the organisation. She claimed that we were belittling her out of jealousy, because none of us had a PhD. She resigned, and her husband came to the office a week later, to castigate us for mistreating his wife.

Self-regulation and shared visions

Initially, there had been no Staff Code of Conduct or other personnel regulations within ZWRCN. Since male-dominant gender ideology has controlled women and dictated their 'needs', we thought that our organisation should challenge such controls; we believed that there was no need to control adults. If members of staff were emotionally linked to the mission, vision, objectives, and strategies of ZWRCN, they would act in the interests of the organisation.

We suggested that if there was a dispute, a dialogue should take place to resolve it. However, in 1994 we were forced to adopt a code of conduct, when an external consultant was invited by us to conduct an assessment of our organisational development. He was horrified that we did not have formal systems in place. We were seen as 'unprofessional' by an outside world which was scrutinising and judging us continuously. The consultant recommended management systems, boundaries of prudence, and a code of ethics to be observed by staff, based on text-book theories of bureaucratic management (internal reports, ZWRCN, 1994).

To the consultant, management was management! Though we modified some of the regulations, some were standard, and meant to protect us in case of dispute, so there was not much we could change. Our lawyers backed up the consultant's advice to conform to established regulations.

The pressure on ZWRCN to conform should be seen in the context of the necessity to relate to donor agencies. In my experience, for most donors, there is only one standard way of doing things. If your organisation deviates, then funding is not forthcoming, regardless of the quality of your work. Consultants hired by donors to evaluate organisations tend to have stereotyped images of what an organisation should be.

However, despite introducing staff regulations, we decided to keep faith with our feminist beliefs by going further than the legal requirements demanded in giving benefits to our staff, to meet what we perceived to be our moral obligations as feminists working together. We were to pay heavily for this. According to the staff regulations, staff members who are on probation do not join our medical aid scheme. However, when a young woman straight from university joined us, we decided to ignore this regulation and put her on the medical scheme while she was still on probation. She was pregnant, and we knew that without medical aid, it would be expensive for her to go for antenatal check-ups.

Unfortunately, we discovered that she was not the right person for the job. We did not confirm her in the post, and terminated her employment. She subsequently took us to court on grounds of unfair dismissal, and her lawyer insisted that she was a permanent member of staff, since we had put her on the medical aid scheme: 'if she had not been confirmed, then why did we put her on medical aid?'. Thus, the lawyer argued, we should have gone through proper dismissal procedures, as is standard when dismissing a permanent member of staff.

Our employee knew the truth, but she decided to use our feminist approach to employment to crucify us. We lost the case, and learnt our lesson the hard way. Nowadays, we may falter here and there, but we have learnt to take staff regulations seriously.

Juggling ideals of sisterhood with 'professional' life

Through deciding to pursue a vision that our staff did not yet share, not only did we find ourselves leading the organisation, but we found ourselves involved in the day-to-day activities of the organisation, on top of our own jobs. We were performing proprietary, supervisory, and operational roles within the organisation. We led very stressful lives.

The conditions under which we were working obliged us to establish a culture of flexible working hours. For founder members, this meant working around the clock. We wanted to ensure the organisation was well established (and anyway, if you are involved in a struggle do you look at your watch?) Most founder members still work 24 hours a day!

However, this willingness to work longer hours did not go down well with some of the staff members. If we were to work effectively, often it meant all of us working late, and sometimes during weekends. We were not unmindful of women's workload, but just thought that they could, once in a while, rest during the week if they needed to, and work odd hours on other days as the situation demanded. (This should be understood in the context of the common availability, in Zimbabwe, of family members to perform domestic work, or affordable domestic workers.)

As well as the commitment to working around the clock to pursue our vision, there was a second commitment: to a feminist vision of women working in sisterhood together. Both these considerations make a division between personal and professional life appear artificial. To maintain morale, we did try very hard to keep the team-spirit going, cooking in our homes and inviting each other to share the food, celebrating each other's birthdays, taking small delicacies from home to the office to share, providing a shoulder to cry on if one of us was victimised by a husband who thought that we were destroying his home.

But always, some hearts were bleeding. Members of staff — and some of our friends — said that despite our claims to being feminists, we were slave-drivers. Some staff started calling us 'Superwomen': a name that came to have negative and derogatory connotations. Some people in the organisation started questioning if ideals of 'sisterhood' were really necessary: 'I come to do my job and I do it well, why should I be forced to be social?' they asked. Such criticisms have a way of taking their toll on an individual as time goes on; and always, it was the same people (especially founder members and a few of the first members of staff) who carried the torch.

Moving towards a 'traditional' culture?

Where is the ZWRCN now in terms of its feminist culture? My feeling is that however much we recognise that the ways of doing things are unjust, we are not only resigning ourselves to living with such traditions but resorting more and more to those ways of doing things.

For example, the organisation has now expanded and the role of the Board been streamlined. However, the implication of a commitment to a feminist culture for the roles and responsibilities of Board Members have not been thought out clearly. As we continue to 'professionalise' the organisation, perhaps we are moving towards a culture of participation: a less politicised concept than that of a feminist culture. We are discovering that it is more peaceful and comfortable to settle for a way of running the organisation which is less threatening to gender relations in the

wider society. Husbands no longer accuse the organisation of breaking up their marriages.

Conclusion: pitfalls, puzzles, and lessons

Can a feminist approach work in a world where nothing else has changed? The process of creating an organisation with a feminist culture turned out to be more complicated than we had anticipated, requiring a reversal of the values and attitudes that most women have since early childhood.

Women grow up believing that having a head of the household is the natural order and a just way of doing things; in the workplace, women and men hold a parallel belief that security comes from rigid structures and systems. The achievement of an alternative culture — in this case, a feminist organisational culture — involves the entire persona of staff-members, not only their time during office hours. Establishing this alternative way of working is a long-term process which demands support: among other things, assistance with reflection on action, and a good deal of counselling. One is preparing people to work in an environment which is not ready for the new culture.

At the inception of ZWRCN, there was little debate about the risks of establishing a 'feminist culture' at work. We were so eager to start real work — and justify receiving donor money — that we did not find the time to arrive at a shared inner vision of the organisation; from there, we could have determined how we were to operate. A feminist culture works if there is understanding of the self, of the need to make choices that may go against cultural and social expectations, and of patterns of behaviour that may create dependence, interdependence, and autonomy within the organisation. A planning exercise would have enabled us to examine how our management styles would compete with our own upbringing.

In the absence of such conscious planning, when we experienced setbacks, we were shattered. The lack of a shared vision has been painful; sometimes heartbreaking. Once, when we were discussing the whole issue of a feminist culture, a member of the team laughed in the most cynical manner possible. Do you know how disempowering such laughter can be? According to her, we were being petty. Challenging accepted ways of doing things demands superhuman commitment and energy. A time came when we could not sustain that amount of energy, experimentation, and uncertainty .

All has not been bleak, though; despite all the pitfalls, our approach of building the capacity of staff in a process of self-education and understanding has had its benefits. Not only did our first programme officer, who was fresh from university, become a strong feminist, but she also developed leadership qualities. She started Zimbabwe's Young Women's Feminist Group, and when she left ZWRCN she continued with her studies in gender and development. She is now employed by UNDP as a Gender and Development Officer. She is also a member of our Board: a good investment for the ZWRCN! Another of the first employees, who started as a cleaner, is now a clerk and able to take on a managerial role. She is an empowered woman: able to hold her own in any argument, and very clear about her rights as a woman. We have witnessed her growth with much pride.

Hope Chigudu is a co-founder, and current Chairperson, of ZWRCN. She describes herself as 'a development entrepreneur and feminist'. Contact details: ZWRCN, 288c Herbert Chitepo Avenue, PO Box 2192, Harare, Zimbabwe. Fax no: 00 263 4 720 331. E-mail: zwrcn@mango.apc.org

References

Chigudu, H (1995) 'Documenting Women's Organizational Experience. The Case of ZWRCN' (unpublished paper).

Connell, R W (1987) *Gender and Power*, Policy Press, Cambridge.

Joseph, S (1996) 'Patriarchy and development in the Arab world', in *Gender and Development*, 4: 2.

Note

1 For the purposes of this paper, I define organisational culture as the way in which an organisation shows and lives out its values, through the way things are done.

AFRA confronts gender issues:

the process of creating a gender strategy

Moya Bydawell

The process of incorporating a gender strategy for its work was not without problems for AFRA. In the South African context, the issues of race and gender can interact to cause conflict and misunderstanding. This article describes how the organisation dealt with the difficulties that had to be overcome in order to develop a common perspective and approach.

The Association for Rural Advancement (AFRA) is an independent rural land service organisation in South Africa, affiliated to the National Land Committee. AFRA is involved in redressing the legacy of unjust land dispensation in the apartheid era. About 450,000 people in rural Natal were forcibly removed from their homes and their land as a consequence of apartheid legislation between 1948 and 1982. AFRA's mission statement emphasises its commitment to working with marginalised groups within communities: these include women, young people, and the 'poorest of the poor'.[1]

Since the first democratically-elected government took power in 1994, and the subsequent removal of apartheid legislation from the statute books, AFRA's work has focused on assisting communities to regain land which they lost through forcible removal or eviction, and on helping communities who have regained

their land, or who are applying for land, to develop the land in a sustainable way. AFRA is concerned to work with communities on ifluencing land reform and the formulation of a just land and agrarian policy for South Africa).

AFRA's work is funded mostly by grants from international donor agencies. For much of AFRA's lifespan, the organisation was run on a voluntary and part-time basis. Gradually, more paid staff have been employed, and staff numbers have increased.

This article recounts part of the organisation's history. Everyone at AFRA has had an opportunity to contribute their views, and to comment on this article before publication, and in this sense, it represents an organisational authorship.[2] Gender as a concept has deep significance, not only for AFRA's development and purpose, but at a personal level for its own staff members. Taking on a gender perspective has brought a recognition that the implications of development work go far beyond the work itself: the issues are conflictual and personal. Within AFRA, we have begun to develop a common perspective and approach. In so doing, we have travelled a long way, and for this reason, AFRA has decided to share its experience of integrating a gender perspective into its activities.

Introducing gender issues into AFRA

The late 1980s saw an increased prominence of gender issues in public debates: within South African politics, in debates on land rights, and within the media. The development of the new Constitution, and equality clauses in the Bill of Rights encouraged those wishing to increase gender-awareness within AFRA, as did the prioritisation of women as a category of land beneficiaries in the government's Land Reform Policy Green Paper.

In 1990, we decided that clarity was needed as to the meaning of 'gender' and its implications for AFRA. We organised a one-day workshop on gender issues for our eight staff, run by a consultant from the Institute of Natural Resources. At this workshop, basic differences emerged, and the concept of working on gender issues was explored for the first time.

Ideas discussed at this first workshop had developed largely without reference to theoretical debates on gender and development; however, they did reflect different positions in those debates. For example, there was disagreement about whether 'gender work' should concentrate on improving women's capacity to do traditionally-defined 'women's work', or if the concept of women's work itself should be challenged, and women enabled to participate fully and equally, at all levels, on their own terms.

The workshop resulted in a recognition of the conflicting views held by staff. Two main issues summarise the turmoil; first, what is meant by 'gender' as a principle? Some participants saw gender issues and feminism as one and the same, and associated them with white, lesbian women. The second issue was the practical implications of using gender analysis in work with grassroots communities. Many of our staff felt this analysis 'had no relationship to lived reality' (internal documents, AFRA), or to the interests expressed by women in the communities with which we work. Women often hold views which are more 'conservative' than the ones held by AFRA staff. For example, if rural women say they want male household heads to hold the title to land, how far should we attempt to influence and change these views? And what would the consequences be if we were to do so? Our conflict, and our confusion over the issues, were so intense that we felt unable to pursue the matter, and the issue of gender was at that stage abandoned by the organisation.

Gender, race, and culture

Later that year, gender issues flared up into the open once more, when a male staff member displayed pin-up posters of scantily-dressed women in one of the offices. Two women staff objected so strongly to the display of the posters that they handed in their resignations.

In terms of racial identity, the structure of authority in AFRA in 1991 reflected the norms of the time: the board and management were all white, the field-workers almost all black. The polarised relations over the gender issue became conflated with racial identity and power-structures. The conflict became so acute, and positions so immovable, that the board was asked to mediate. (This showed the seriousness of the situation, as the board is not usually involved in internal issues.)

The conflict became more bitter when the man — a white male field worker — who had put up the posters was asked by the board to resign, which resulted in his close friend following suit. After the board's investigation, it was felt that the poster issue had become a flashpoint for deeper conflicts within AFRA; for many, the issues represented by the term 'gender' were experienced as an assault on their race and cultural identity.

It is now recognised that, although there were very real gender issues at stake, they could not be addressed while another issue of identity and diversity — that of race — was so pivotal to the organisation's culture and ability to function. Subsequently, a myth has developed in AFRA about the 1990 incident: the posters are said to have shown bare-breasted Msinga[3] 'maidens', rather than 'pin-ups' of white naked women. Since bare-breastedness holds no sexual significance for Zulu people, this mythical reconstruction of what actually happened poses interesting questions for the linkages between race, culture, and feminism.

Staff questions on gender

Some staff reported feeling ambivalence towards the issue of gender, in comparison to an acute awareness of racial problems within the organisation. For example, among the issues which were explored at the time was the valuation of certain types of work. It was felt by some staff that the organisation placed a higher value on the thinking and research work carried out by white management, than on the fieldwork, which was carried out by black workers, who were at that time all men. There was a sense among some staff that fieldwork had been devalued to the status of 'a translation service' (internal documents).

Staff interviewed for this article said that they had consciously avoided taking up the issue of gender because of the conflict and bitterness it provoked. Those who took up the issue often found themselves isolated. Other staff said that they were committed to integrating gender into their work, but lacked the knowledge to do this. Many felt that their concerns had not been properly dealt with, because of the conflict and confusion within the organisation at that time.

How far could, or should, AFRA go in taking forward the issue of gender? Many staff felt that to do so would involve the organisation interfering in people's private and personal lives. Did AFRA have the skills and resources to cope with the conflict which gender issues could raise in communities? Some staff feared that it could jeopardise AFRA's central focus on land. Others asked whether AFRA staff had the moral right to interfere in rural African culture.

Gender issues in the wider community

In 1992, changes took place in the external environment. A community-based fieldworker, Mam Lydia Kompe, (now a member of the South African parliament) introduced gender issues onto the agenda of the National Land Committee. Mam Lydia was a black woman, and this meant that gender could no longer be easily dismissed as a white, 'Western', or lesbian issue.

However, in AFRA, the issues of race and gender remained linked. The implementation of gender-training workshops, and the design of strategies for gender work, were carried out mainly by white women development workers, and responsibility for AFRA's work on gender was given to a white woman. She and other staff agree that, as a result of the race issue, and the implications of gender being seen as a white Western and invasive concern, she was unable to make much progress. AFRA attempted to deal with the racial conflict within it, organising a staff workshop facilitated by a local psychologist. Gender was discussed as being part of the problem, but was not a primary focus.

In 1993, the National Land Committee Gender Task Team organised a participatory methodology workshop, in which AFRA staff and NLC staff were to consider the integration of gender issues into their work. AFRA, and many other affiliated NLC organisations, had no women field workers at that time. Thus, most workshop participants were men. The workshop was conflictual from the beginning. Suspicion and resistance were expressed, both to the issues, and the workshop process itself. Once again, anger about race dynamics became a pivotal focus and many voiced their feeling that gender was foreign to the culture of South Africa, being a white Western issue. This was only to be expected, as once again the facilitators were white women!

Soon after this a Fieldworkers' Forum was established, both within AFRA itself, and within the whole of the NLC, to deal with the dissent surrounding power and race. AFRA was considered to be the first organisation within the NLC to have dealt openly with both race and gender issues.

Questioning the staffing structure of AFRA

In 1993, an external evaluation of AFRA brought all the same tensions to the surface. The interconnected issues of race and gender were still causing conflict, not only within AFRA but within the NLC as a whole, with many people threatening to resign over the valuation of categories of work, and corresponding racial and gender divisions. Within AFRA, this led to the reassessment of its staffing structure.

It was decided that for AFRA to survive as an effective organisation, this structure had to be reorganised to become more democratic and racially representative. In addition, the fact that most employees were men was identified as a major obstacle to implementation of any integrated gender work. Fieldwork had always been an exclusively male domain, whilst women tended to be involved in administration and research. Women fieldworkers would have a different approach.

At the time of writing, there are four black women fieldworkers (one of whom is also a co-ordinator of a unit), three black women administrators, two white women co-ordinators, one white woman staff member handling media issues, one black woman resource centre manager, three black male co-ordinators, five male black fieldworkers, one Indian male staff member, one black male administrator, and a white male director.

The role of gender specialists

In 1995, AFRA appointed its first woman fieldworker, and also a gender specialist, who would deal with aspects of women's empowerment within the target communities, as well as raising the issue within AFRA. The appointment of the gender specialist became a cause of further contention. Some staff felt that the gender specialist was now 'doing gender', and this meant that they were not to get involved with the issues themselves; while many others resented the appointment, feeling that they had been integrating gender issues all along. Resentment was fuelled by a lack of confidence in the appointment process: some staff claimed that there had been insufficient consultation within the organisation, although others said that consultation did take place (personal communications).

Since the appointment of the gender specialist, there has been a new clarity of approach to fieldwork. Much of AFRA's work continues to be concerned with women's rights, particularly in relation to land, and about dealing with issues defined by women as obstacles to their attainment of rights, for example, domestic violence. Yet disagreements continue about the choice of issues to address, in AFRA and the communities with which it works.

The gender specialist became the target of gender-related tension. According to her, this often took the form of verbal harassment. The organisation again became polarised. This was especially destructive to existing good relations, and spilled over into other structures and issues within the organisation. The co-ordinator of the unit in which the gender specialist was working brought the new problems to the management committee; it was hoped that a gender workshop convened by an outside consultant would bring fresh insights, from a position of neutrality.

Cracking the issue of identity through training

The facilitator of this workshop, Mel Adisu, a black Ethiopian man, approached the issues in a different way, being aware of the resistance to gender as an issue because of problems to do with race in the South African context, and the association of gender with white, Western feminism. The purpose of this workshop was made explicit: to create an atmosphere in which all participants could examine their roles, responsibilities, and relationships with others in the organisation; and to examine the organisation's values and goals.

Methodology
The workshop opened with an initial agreement that opinions expressed would

remain confidential; individuals are working in a difficult environment, and would not have felt free to speak openly and honestly without such a confidentiality clause. The workshop included trust-building and team-building exercises, many of which had a strong psychological slant, encouraging people to express their perceptions of the issues, their ways of behaving, and what informs these. There were also exercises to encourage creativity and free communication, including artwork and movement.

Outcome
Workshop participants realised that sensitivity was required in addressing gender issues, but that there should at the same time be no concessions on the commitment to promote the rights of women. These rights have been enshrined in South Africa's new Constitution, as an aspect of human rights. Taking on a commitment to gender thus profoundly affects work with communities, and also challenges an organisation's internal culture.

Mel Adisu emphasised the fact that an organisation such as AFRA, which is involved in social change, necessarily operates at levels which are informed by the personal beliefs and feelings of its members. Personal ideals are a driving force behind change, and the personal and political positions of people within the organisation thus need to be acknowledged. It was seen that in order to create change within the organisation, trust, and acceptance were needed, so that people could express their true feelings and fears about the issues.

A significant issue identified by participants was the ease with which people adopt the correct language to fit in with the trends in the organisation. This can happen without the meanings of the language being internalised. The mismatch between what we say and what we believe creates intense stress and confusion, and affects the organisation's ability to deal with similar conflicts within the communities with which it works.

Finally, and most importantly, one positive result of the workshop was that participants seemed to move toward a shared common understanding of 'gender' as an aspect of social differentiation, and as being concerned with the relationship between men and women, rather than being a 'women's issue'.

Moving forward: the aftermath

After this workshop, the organisation committed itself to taking work on gender issues forward in an integrated and inclusive way, by developing an integrated gender strategy, which was to take cognisance of all positions, needs, and fears. All members of AFRA will be involved in the design of the strategy.

Our struggle to understand and take up gender inequity as a central feature of our work, and the conflicts that we have had, need to be acknowledged and affirmed as a necessary process, which we have as a group been courageous and honest in confronting. We must remember all this, if we are to alleviate the remaining tensions concerning gender in AFRA, and to define the roles and functions of staff regarding gender issues.

We cannot pretend that we have found a solution to the complexity of the issue; this complexity is one which is reflected in society at large. Perhaps we can say that the outcome thus far is a sense of acceptance of our individuality, and the need for us to be non-judgemental of other people's positions. The conflict and discomfort around gender within organisations should perhaps be accepted as integral and positive, as the issue is concerned with change.

Moya Bydawell is serving a six-month internship at AFRA, 123 Loop Street, Pietermaritzburg 3201 Tel: 0331-457607; e-mail: afra@wn.apc.org

References

Marcus, T. (1995) *Kwa-Zulu Natal Synthesis Report*, Land and Agricultural Policy Centre. Pietermaritzburg.

Notes

1   Although it is often stated that women are the poorest of the poor, the picture is more complex in the communities in which AFRA works; rather than being synonymous, these groups overlap. For example, recent research from the Centre for Social and Development Studies at Durban University indicates that while the poorest category of people (urban and rural) are single mothers, women pensioners are often wealthier than young men (personal communication).

2   To allow me to draft this article, various staff members were interviewed. They represented a range of views and positions within the organisation, and were consulted on the understanding of confidentiality and inclusion in the process of approving the article. I have also drawn on internal documents, including people's personal reports, as well as minutes of meetings. Finally, I refer to the 'time line', which was the result of a staff focus meeting, where everyone contributed to an exercise to get a sense of AFRA's position and history in terms of gender. This enabled the contextualisation of the issue and events in terms of macro, community and personal influences.

3   Msinga refers to a former 'homeland' area

Promoting women entrepreneurs in Lebanon:

the experience of UNIFEM

Randa Husseini

This article gives a personal perspective on a programme in which UNIFEM has been involved, which aimed to strengthen the capabilities of governmental and non-governmental organisations working on micro-enterprise, and to make the services they provide sensitive to gender concerns.

The work of the United Nations Development Fund for Women (UNIFEM) in West Asia started in 1994 with the setting-up of the regional office in Amman-Jordan, and the Fund's direct implementation of a regional programme to strengthen institutions for the development of women-owned enterprises in Jordan, Syria and Lebanon. Since 1976, when its work began formally, UNIFEM has supported more than 50 projects in the region. Our ultimate aim was to integrate women workers in the informal sector into mainstream economic development. Emphasis was placed on the incorporation of gender analysis in programme planning. Gender analysis is a very new concept in Lebanon.

The Gulf War in 1991 increased economic hardship, and in response to this, towards the end of 1991, UNIFEM decided to promote women's entrepreneurship The decision followed a number of needs-assessment missions, and thorough discussions with national organisations. We found evidence that, despite the fact that women's participation in the monetised labour force has increased,[1] it is limited by the availability of jobs open to women, and by women's need to balance economic activity with family responsibilities. In response to the unfriendliness of the formal sector, many women turn to the informal sector, where business is precarious, earnings are often very low, and where there is a virtually complete lack of support services and benefits.

Assessing the situation

In the first phase of the programme, we identifyied, surveyed, and assessed the existing organisations which shared our concern, and our target groups of beneficiaries. We needed to quickly define the needs and problems to be addressed at both micro-, and macro-level. We became aware of the scarcity of studies on women and work in the region, and the lack of reliable information on women's status in the economy in general, and their role in the private sector.

To fill this information gap, we analysed the available statistics, which were somewhat out-of-date, allying this to empirical information on the problems and needs of the micro-enterprise sector. We obtained this through a survey, using rapid appraisal techniques, and interviews with about 100 women entrepreneurs, gathered at random from poor rural and peri-urban areas of Lebanon.

Investigating credit

Not only did we need information on those who would potentially be interested in our programme; we also needed to find out about the credit provision and financial services for women which already existed. One of the objectives of the UNIFEM programme is to expand the availability of financial services to low-income women entrepreneurs, through negotiating agreements with national financial institutions. For this purpose, we needed to know what was happening before our intervention.

We carried out a survey of almost all non-traditional credit programmes, and a sample survey of the formal financial institutions, to measure the effectiveness of the available range of credit support for women. The survey included seven banks, none of which had gender-desegregated data. When we asked the banks about the percentage of women who used their services, they replied that the financial services do not take into account the sex of the applicant. Nevertheless, when they reviewed their files, they found that this implied impartiality masked a very low percentage of female borrowers — between 1 and 3 per cent. (Subsequently, the banks admitted that our question had been a valid one!)

Gender training

Working on gender issues is made particularly difficult in our region as the word 'gender' cannot readily be translated into Arabic, and gender analysis was a new concept for all development workers — even the UNIFEM staff in Lebanon. Most of the organisations (including those who are members of the Lebanese Women's Council[2])which have been providing relief during the war, need support and assistance in capacity-building for post-war development activities, including the promotion of a gender perspective in their mainstream development work.

Thus, the UNIFEM project organised a gender-awareness workshop, which was attended by 26 representatives of government and NGOs, including the banking sector. Only three men were present; one of them was so uneasy that he sent his apologies and did not attend the second day of the workshop.

Strategic planning

After these preparatory steps, a strategic planning workshop (SPW) was attended by over 30 national institutions and UN agencies, some of which were represented by top-ranking officials; and also by women entrepreneurs, who shared their experiences with the representatives.

It appears that for most women entrepreneurs, the services they needed were simply not available. If they existed, women were either unaware of them, or they were not easily accessible. Representatives of the organisations discussed in their turn the problems they experienced in service delivery. As well as a shortage of human and financial resources, the various institutions delivering training, finance, and marketing and business-counselling services, mentioned the need for their programmes to be updated and upgraded, in order to adapt them to the changing technological and economic needs, and to make them available and affordable to women entrepreneurs.

For example, the meeting heard that NGOs and government ministries were training women in inappropriate skills: traditionally 'female' activities, such as the production of handicrafts. Despite the fact that women received some help in marketing their products, they were not very successful, and this approach seemed unsustainable.

The SPW was expected to yield detailed sub-sector work-plans for training, marketing, credit, production, business-counselling and advocacy; but because of the above-mentioned constraints, and the lack of a tradition of co-ordination, the workshop did not succeed in finding areas of cooperation among the organisations, or developing plans for future work.

Study-tours to share ideas

In the second phase of the project, UNIFEM set up a study-tour to the Philippines and Thailand, with the intention of giving representatives from academia, government, and NGOS (including a representative of a training centre affiliated to a major NGO, and from a rural grassroots organisation) the opportunity to look at other models of providing institutional support to small and micro-enterprises. We hoped that this experience would help to promote a common vision as to the next steps of the UNIFEM programme, in terms of putting together a detailed plan of action and implementation with governmental institutions and NGOs. Some participants found the study-tour visits inspirational.

Another initiative involving representatives of major credit institutions was facilitated by the UNIFEM Technical Section. This was a global workshop on credit, held in Amman, which provided a good opportunity to share ideas across the regions of the world on income-generation, and for training in gender and credit, and advocacy for women's access to credit.

The demand for resources

After the workshop, we decided to implement a second phase of data collection; a survey to assess micro-entrepreneurs' demands for financial and other services. We interviewed a randomly selected group of programme participants of two major credit schemes, and an equal number of randomly selected micro-entrepreneurs who did not participate in any NGO programme, but lived in the regions where the NGOs operated.

The survey results confirmed that women were found mainly in the less profitable economic sectors, producing handicrafts and food products or running small service or trading companies. When asked about the reason for establishing enterprises, 8.8 per cent of men said that gaining independence was an important factor; however this did not seem to be of such concern for women — only 2.2 per cent of them stated that it was.

Examining the sources of start-up finance, we found that 1.2 per cent of women got loans from banks, compared to 4.8 per cent of men. In addition, men were found to have been in operation on average twice as long as women, and they also spent more time on business activities. This is due to the unpaid domestic work and child-care normally done by women.

Looking at the size of the enterprises, male-operated enterprises were larger than female-operated ones, and more male entrepreneurs were previously employees of and received training through the family business compared to female entrepreneurs. Only 17 per cent of women registered their businesses, compared to 44 per cent of men. Most women reported that it was not necessary to register their businesses; this is because about half of the women in the sample ran their businesses from home.

When both women and men were asked to specify the kind of training they needed, and whether they were ready to pay for training or business-counselling services, they did not know what was needed, nor what was available, and were not very keen on paying for such services.

Gender and the national employment census

The lack of statistics and other data can only be overcome if gender-sensitive questions are built in to future surveys from the start. Concurrently with doing our own survey outlined above, in 1994 the UNIFEM team contacted the Ministry of Industry, and succeeded in influencing it to include gender concerns in the design of the second phase of the National Census of the industrial sector.

We also carried out a number of other activities at many levels, for example, discussing with the Industrialists' Association possible ways of extending their services to small industrialists. In co-operation with UNIDO (United Nations Industrial Development Organisation), we surveyed the sub-contracting phenomenon, particularly in the tailoring, shoe industry, and canned food sectors; and organised with ESCWA (United Nations Economic and Social Commission for Western Asia) a workshop for introducing the concept of 'small business incubators' as a means of promoting entrepreneurship among women. (This inovolves the provision of common premises, logistics, and technical support for a group of small business enterpreneurs, who pay a reduced fee for these facilities.)

The lessons learned from this stage of our work were very important in shaping our subsequent actions. First, the idea behind the programme was innovative;

there were no projects or related programmes for the support of small and micro-enterprises, and more specifically to support women in these activities. Private professional associations, such as the Chamber of Commerce, Industry and Agriculture (less than 1 per cent of whose members are women) or the Industrialists Association (15 women out of a total of 1500) were directed towards men, and relatively large enterprises. Even though there is extensive information available about the private sector and financial market, there is hardly any gender-desegregated information.

Second, the government ministries concerned were overwhelmed by the demands created by reconstruction of damaged physical infrastructure, and due to the war and emigration, were short of qualified staff to cater for new programmes. In addition, government budget constraints have reduced the funding available for programmes involving women and for social-service support programmes.

Third, lack of credit is one of the main obstacles that limit the ability of women entrepreneurs to develop their businesses; as we found, banking regulations discriminate against low-income entrepreneurs. In addition to this, the problem of access to credit by women is compounded by their lack of information, the male-oriented collateral requirements, the complicated procedures, and the lack of confidence on the part of women.

Fourth, we encountered difficulties in promoting co-operation among organisations and their representatives. The funds that we had for the programme were modest, and could only be used to initiate the different processes, but would not stretch to support them.

Last, but not least, we realised that we ought to deal first with the problems faced by poor women who own and operate micro-enterprises in the most disadvantaged areas of the country.

'Mainstreaming' gender

In the third phase of our programme, we decided to channel our programme activities mainly through the Ministry of Social Affairs, which is the principal body in Lebanon carrying out support activities directed to women. It deals with the poorest segments of the population, through its Community Development Centres, or through NGOs. It is the only ministry which has a female Director, and was the first to establish a department for women's affairs, although this is not functioning yet. The Ministry showed interest in our programme, and committed some of its remaining 1995 budget to it; subsequently, the programme attracted the support of the UNDP office in Beirut.[3]

The programme is now assisting the Ministry of Social Affairs to adapt to the post-war situation. The intention is to develop the Ministry's capacity to train women to establish small businesses, helping them to identify and develop ideas, and transform the ideas into viable enterprises, in addition to providing counselling on legal matters, marketing, and credit sources. Our experience of working with the Ministry was quite successful, in spite of some constraints, which included subsidising the very low wages of social workers involved in the programme, or having to appeal upwards to the Director to overcome bureaucratic obstacles. These constraints are outweighed by the real commitment of the Ministry to the programme's objectives, and to the development of women's entrepreneurship.

The programme is computerising a number of Community Development Centres, and staff have been trained in data collection, analysis, monitoring, and the evaluation of the impact of programme activities on the target group. The programme will also support the Social Services Training Centre, in the updating of its curriculum, and the incorporation of entrepreneurship and gender analysis units in the training of social workers.

During 1996, and due to the very good outreach capacity of the Ministry of Social Affairs, the project was able to develop a core of trainers at the Ministry, to provide technical support to the UNIFEM programme in Syria, and to complete the training of 209 Lebanese women who will soon announce the formation of the first businesswomen's club in Lebanon.

In conclusion, despite the newness of the concept of gender in Lebanon, the need for gender training, and making gender-desegregated data available, we expect that a knowledge of gender-related employment issues, and the use of gender-specific analysis, will become integral to the Ministry's programme and project planning. Through sharing our experience of work at community level, we hope to encourage government institutions and NGOs to integrate gender issues into their planning and structure.

Randa Husseini has been the Programme Manager for UNIFEM in Lebanon since 1994. She trained as an agricultural engineer and previously worked with FAO in Zimbabwe. Contact: Unifil House, Bir Hassan, POB 11-3216, Beirut, Lebanon.
e-mail: ihh@inco.com.lb

Notes

1 This is attributed to many factors including a decrease in fertility rates, increase in school enrolments, expanding urbanisation and the prevailing economic crisis worsened by the decline in migrant remittances.
2 This is an umbrella group of 132 Lebanese NGOs, which all run programmes targeting women.
3 The programme is now supported by UNDP, UNIFEM, Friedrich Ebert Foundation, ESCWA, and AGFUND.

Women's rights, the family, and organisational culture:

a Lesotho case study

Elizabeth Everett

This article discusses the work of Lesotho Save the Children (LSC) in caring for girls who have suffered sexual abuse within their families. Support takes the form of providing refuge in the 'substitute family' setting of a Children's Village in Maseru, Lesotho's capital, where counselling and rehabilitation is offered.

Current international and national commitments to address gender issues, including violence against women and girls, encourage programme work of this nature. At country level, growing attention is being paid to women's rights, by Basotho women themselves, and the government. Lesotho has, in common with many other countries, in both South and North, accepted appropriate United Nations conventions on the rights of women and children. Lesotho signed up to the UN Convention on the Rights of the Child in 1991, under its former military government; while the Convention on All Forms of Discrimination Against Women has been signed during the past year (Shoeshoe 1996). Donor agencies are ensuring that these issues remain on the government agenda: 'there are four major issues facing the Government of Lesotho at this time ... and perhaps the most important [the government] must address itself to is the rights of women and girls' (Kakonge, quoted in *Lesotho Today*, 13 September 1996).

The organisational agenda of Lesotho Save the Children (LSC) is influenced by that of the International Save the Children Alliance (ISCA).[1] The policies of ISCA clearly define the rights of women and girls: 'Save the Children sees the role and status of women as critical to social progress and to the fulfilment of children's rights. Save the Children pays special attention to the needs of women and girls' (Save the Children Charter Article 9, 1991).

However, as gender and development researchers have emphasised in many different organisational contexts, while policies of donors and governments are invaluable in setting out principles, it is often extremely difficult to put them into practice in different contexts. Such policies may be perceived as clashing with location-specific views on traditional culture and the family, through exposing issues which were formerly kept within the private sphere (Schuler 1992).

Organisational culture is a key factor in ensuring the success of such work. As I attempt to show, LSC's organisational culture is rooted strongly in its social context, and reflects sets of norms from notions of 'traditional' Sesotho culture, and from the post-colonial, paternalistic attitudes of the organisation's British founders. This article explores the implications of these considerations, for LSC's work, and internal structure.

LSC's evolving culture

LSC was founded in 1964, by a group of English expatriates living in Lesotho, who responded to a perceived need to provide institutionally-based care for boys whose families were unable to cope with their disabilities, the majority of which were caused by poliomyelitis. From 1964 to 1990, after a major review took place, the programme work of LSTC was focused solely on the needs of boys and young men, in line with the view of LSC's founder, Winifred Coaker, who chaired the organisation until her resignation in 1989: 'Our policy is to educate every boy who comes to us for residential care, regardless of age, either academically or vocationally, until he is equipped to earn a living. We know that if these boys remained in their homes they would have no future' (Lesotho Save the Children 1989i). In the mid-1970s a second institution for boys was opened, for children who were believed to be abandoned orphans.

In 1990, major policy reviews of LSC were undertaken after pressure was placed on the organisation from a number of external and internal stakeholders. Externally, these included ISCA, and international donors. The review was supported fully by the two chairpersons who succeeded the founder upon her resignation, shortly before her death, in 1989. Internal anxiety about the aims and philosophies informing the organisation was fuelled by the election to the management and central committees of several feminists, who questioned the emphasis on caring for boys.

The rationale for this emphasis is on record in the annual reports of LSC throughout the 1970s and 1980s: 'We are sometimes asked why we neglect the welfare of girls and seem to concentrate our efforts only on boys ... Our decision to assist boys was based on a social situation that is strange to this part of the world. Girls receive longer and better formal education than boys and a destitute girl will always find a family eager to care for her. Even within the family, girls receive better care than boys. The system of bride price is one of the foundations of our society and a family with a daughter can expect to receive livestock when she marries ... but whatever the means of payment a healthy, educated daughter is a sound investment for the future and as such she will be cared for and receive preference when the family's scarce resources are shared. And so it is the boys who are neglected and abandoned, and we have made it our responsibility to care for them in whatever way we can' (Lesotho Save the Children 1989ii).

The language used here reflects, strikingly, confidence in the ability of an organisation founded and headed by expatriates to recognise the realities of life for Basotho people living in poverty, and their belief in their right to formulate an organisational response.

Redetermining LSC's organisational mandate

The first decision of the 1990 Review was to close the home for 'orphaned' boys, and send them back to their families. Investigations had revealed that almost all of the boys who were resident at the time of the review (and probably the vast majority who had spent time there over the years) were from poor families, but had neither been orphaned nor abandoned. In many cases, the death of a parent, usually a father, had altered the family financial situation dramatically, and instead of relying on the support of the extended family, the surviving parent sought help from LSC. Previously, these facts were not made explicit, despite LSC staff and management witnessing the exodus of 'orphans' during school holidays (personal experience).

A second decision, to close the home for disabled boys, was more difficult. Both Basotho and expatriates working in the organisation have unquestioningly accepted the notion that the best place for a child is, by definition, at home with his or her family (personal experience). Yet the decision was a difficult one, as this assumption has not in the past been made so readily for disabled children.

After consultation with the government's Department of Social Welfare, it was decided by LSC that the former institution for disabled boys — which took the form of a 'village' on the outskirts of Maseru, Lesotho's capital — should now become a place of safety for children of both sexes, who are in need of care and protection. Within a very short period of time, the boys were replaced by a mixed intake, with a high proportion of girls. Many of these are the victims of physical and sexual abuse by family members. The myth of the earlier days of LSC, that girls were well-cared for within the family, has been fundamentally questioned by our first-hand experience of caring for girls who have suffered terrible oppression within their extended family.

Work with victims of abuse

The girls placed at LSC's village by the Department of Social Welfare have all suffered very badly; many of them are injured physically, and all are injured psychologically. The common experience is of over-work, and abuse within and outside their parental home.

Abuse outside includes the practice of placing the daughters of poor family members within the households of wealthier branches of the family, as domestic labour (Shoeshoe 1991). The understanding is that young girls placed into service in this way will serve all the family's needs. This practice potentially exposes young girls to abuse of all kinds from adults of both sexes, to whom they are often only distantly related. The extent of rape and sexual molestation within these arrangements can only be guessed at, although empirical evidence of this has been gained from girls taken into the Children's Village (personal experience). Typically, it is only when the situation escalates to become intolerable that family members or, in some cases, the authorities, intervene.

One of the female rape victims who came into our care at the age of 12 had been returned, by the police, to the care of her uncle, on three previous occasions. She would probably still be there, if she had not been discovered by an LSC social worker, huddling in the back of an office at the police station in a remote town. When the social worker enquired of the police why she was there, he was told that they would have to return her to the uncle, as they did not know where else to take her.

This girl remains in the care of LSC, until other family members can assure us that she will be safe with them, and until she is psychologically able to cope with life within her family. In our experience, it is dangerous to rely upon assurance by family members as to the safety of abused girls who are returned to the care of their relations. There are many instances where girls have been returned to distant relatives of the abusing male, under the care of a woman, only to have him arrive on the doorstep, and demand that she is returned to him (personal communication).

Challenging the personal/professional divide

A reluctance to discuss sexual issues is widespread throughout contemporary Lesotho. Sex is not readily spoken of, either publicly or in private, especially in the presence of the young. This discomfort around acknowledging and discussing sex extends to staff entrusted with the care of rape victims in LSC. During discussions with the supervisor at the Children's Village, soon after the organisational emphasis changed and abused girls had started to arrive, it came to light that the staff were dealing with the rape victims in the same way as they would have done if they were their own children, saying to them: 'Do not talk about it, and try and forget that it happened.'

With no sex education, many of the girls who were virgins until the assault had no idea what was being done to them, or of the possible consequences. All they knew was that it did not feel right (confidential case reports, LSC 1992). Among several young girls who were experiencing nightmares, one believed that there was a snake inside her, as she had seen the 'snake' that had penetrated her (ibid.).

Great emphasis has been placed on staff training to enable staff to overcome their own reticence so that they can offer comfort and counselling to the girls in their care. Our counsellor now holds weekly meetings with the staff to reinforce the idea that sexual abuse is morally wrong, and a criminal act. Talking openly about sex was a new experience for them, and to articulate hostility towards the male perpetrators of rape and abuse was challenging and frightening for staff themselves. Coercive sex is a part of many women's sexual experience in Lesotho, and it is often the prelude to marriage when the prospective bride is kidnapped and raped by her bridegroom (personal communication, June 1993).

Sex education for staff

The social norms of reticence on a subject are reinforced by the logical outcome of these norms: namely, lack of knowledge on the part of staff. One member of staff who was a newly-trained counsellor worked with staff, who told her that it was difficult for them to talk about sex and reproduction with young girls, as they had so little understanding themselves.

When the Lesotho Planned Parenthood Federation (LPPF) offered to visit LSC staff to discuss sexual health and related issues, the offer was initially rejected by staff. Younger women said that they did not wish to attend as the older women would regard them as whores, for being interested in contraception; older women said that it would not be right for the younger women to hear about contraception, and they themselves did not need to know any more. At the time, I was chairperson of the organisation; in that capacity, I took responsibility for inviting the representative anyway, claiming that I needed to know what she had to say. While the staff were initially embarrassed, most were, ultimately, attentive. When I purchased some condoms, and offered to pay for any contraception that women were interested in, I subsequently received a modest bill from the LPPF.

Critically, in assessing our progress, we have to consider both what women say and do when men are not around, and what actually happens when the men are there to assert their authority. The women who told me that they would insist on their husbands using condoms when they returned from the mines in South Africa, all sheepishly told me after the holiday that they had not been brave enough to ask them when it came to the point.

Standing up to abuse by challenging male authority is never easy; yet the LSC staff are now beginning to accept that rape of young girls by family members is unacceptable. Case meetings have become less constrained; women staff eventually felt able to express their feelings towards the male perpetrators of the abuse, without fear that male colleagues would understand this as a personal attack.

LSC can only continue to educate and encourage girls and women to say no to sexual violence, no to abuse of their daughters, and no to the unequal distribution of labour within the family and the home. A long way down the road is the need for further work on challenging the negative aspects of the ideal of the 'traditional' family, and the oppression of women and children which is hidden within it.

Gender issues in the daily life of the institution

Currently, the organisational structure at the children's village is constantly being re-worked, as staff are encouraged to examine their own ideas about gender roles, in their work with the children, and in the structure of the organisation itself.

Gender issues in the staff structure

Since LSC has aimed to provide an alternative 'family' for its children, it has employed women in jobs which are a logical extension of their unpaid work within the household. The ironic result has been that even when LSC was an organisation which focused specifically on providing care for boys, the staff employed by LSC were predominantly strong, capable women.

However, it is a commonly-noted feature of gender relations in Lesotho that many women are *de facto* heads of household, and a high proportion of them receive education and go on to formal employment, due to the large number of men who are absent at work in the South African mines (Wahlstrom 1990); yet, within the family, women are not seen as having any true decision-making power, despite the reality of life without men as a result of the migrant labour system; decisions are often deferred until the man returns on leave, however impractical this may be (Gordon 1981).

In our own staffing structures, we are attempting where possible to challenge the notion that caring roles are 'women's work'. For a period, LSC employed a male social worker; however, this is less challenging to gender stereotyping than it may appear at first, since men are likely to be attracted to 'professional' caring roles with responsibility and status involved. M, a male social worker employed by LSC during the early 1990's, combined a caring role with strict discipline, contravening the rules prohibiting beating the children. He refused to take instructions from his female supervisor on the grounds that he was a professional and she was not. She in her turn reported that she could not control him 'because he was a man' (personal communication, 1993).

The gardener at the children's village falls into the role of care-giver, without overlaying this with the male role of violent 'disciplinarian'. All the gardeners LSC has employed over the years have developed relationships with the children similar to that of the house mothers. Perhaps if you care for plants, caring for children comes naturally!

We plan to recruit new house parents in 1997, and want at least one of these to be a man, but there is disagreement among the governing committee as to whether this man should take on the same role as his female colleagues, or be a 'house father' with a role distinct from that of the house mothers. Some women on the committee are horrified at the idea of a man doing 'women's work', although they themselves are professionals — one is a doctor — whose careers were until recently seen as male occupations.

Work with the children

In our work with the children, the division of labour along traditional lines is being challenged; all children have domestic duties to perform, and staff are asked to recognise that it is possible for boys and girls to do the same work. The rotas that are drawn up ensure that boys and girls get equal time doing the tasks that are traditionally reserved for the opposite sex.

When this was first suggested, one member of staff summed up resistance to challenging gender norms: 'We would be making life hard for the children when they returned to their families, as no parent would accept a boy who washed dishes and swept the floor' (staff meeting 1991). It was initially hard to find tasks for the girls to do that were traditionally the domain of boys; this underlined the fact that all domestic work — including agricultural tasks and all sewing and knitting — are considered to be female responsibilities. The only task that it was agreed was a responsibility of the boys was feeding the dog!

Perhaps the best that can be said for the LSC Children's Village is that it enables children to form close bonds with children from outside their family structure, and to experience a less oppressive life, even if only for a short period. For feminists in LSC, including myself, a major element of this experience should be of equality between girls and boys, women and men.

Elizabeth Everett trained as a teacher. She has lived in Lesotho and worked with LSC since 1980. She is on the management committee and was chairperson from 1991-5. As a feminist, her concern has always been to promote the rights of women and girls. PO Box 964, Maseru 100, Lesotho. Fax (266) 316912.

References

Gordon, E (1981) 'An analysis of the impact of labour migration on the lives of women in Lesotho', *Journal of Development Studies* 17: 3.

Lesotho Save the Children (i), *Quarterly Newsletter*, January 1989.

Lesotho Save the Children (ii), *Chairman's Report* 1989.

Kakonge, J account of an address by J Kakonge, Senior Representative, UNDP, at the launch of the Human Development Report, quoted in *Lesotho Today*, 13 September 1996.

Schuler M *Freedom from Violence: Women's Strategies from around the World*, UNIFEM 1992.

Shoeshoe i; 1:3, Ministry of Information and Broadcasting, Maseru, Lesotho, Early Spring 1991.

Shoeshoe ii; 3:2, February 1996.

Wahlstrom, A *A Lesotho Gender Analysis* SIDA, 1990

Notes

1 Lesotho Save the Children is not at present a member of ISCA, although it is hoped that this association — which has existed throughout most of the organisation's history — will soon be re-formed. LSC was suspended from ISTC in 1995, principally because of a failure to submit audited accounts. However, a number of problems and ethical concerns were also highlighted by the Executive Committee of ISTC, including the issue of a change of focus from a care giver to a development organisation focusing on capacity-building. The majority of the members of the organisation do not support this change of direction, as we believe that we must continue to respond to the requests for assistance that we receive, even if this is seen as an outdated mode of response.

Making the Human Development Index (HDI) gender-sensitive

Shalendra D Sharma

The Human Development Index (HDI) has become a widely used measure for understanding patterns of socio-economic development. This article argues that it could be greatly improved by incorporating sex-disaggregated data, to reveal the different socio-economic contributions and situations of men and women within each country.

The Human Development Index (HDI) was introduced in 1990 by the United Nations Development Programme (UNDP). Unlike the narrow GNP measure (which is based solely on income), the HDI includes three key components, longevity, knowledge, and income, which are combined into a composite human development index to arrive at an 'average deprivation index'. Longevity is measured by life-expectancy at birth as the sole unadjusted indicator. Knowledge is measured by two stock variables: adult literacy and mean years of schooling. The measure of educational achievement is adjusted by assigning a weight of two-thirds to literacy and one-third to mean years of schooling. For income, the HDI is based on the premise of diminishing returns. So, the higher the income relative to the poverty level, the more sharply the diminishing returns affect the contribution of income to human development. In other words, unlike GNP, the HDI measures income by purchasing power, based on real GDP per capita adjusted for the local cost of living or 'purchasing power parity'.

While no single index could ever completely measure the complexity of human development, the HDI offers an alternative to GNP and to the neoclassical measure of 'consumer utility' by capturing levels of human development within countries and measuring relative socio-economic progress. Hence, the HDI not only enables policy-makers to evaluate development over time, and to determine priorities for policy intervention, it also permits comparisons of the experiences of individual countries.

Nevertheless, the HDI has some major flaws. It is well known that an overall development index can conceal the reality that particular groups within a country enjoy very different levels of socio-economic development: men and women, for example, or racial and ethnic groups, regions, and social classes. Unfortunately, the HDI has not adequately incorporated these variables. In particular, it does not reveal how gender disparities affect human development. This is a significant weakness, since global macro- and micro-data indicate that males generally fare better than females on almost every socio-economic indicator, within both industrialised and developing countries (Boserup, 1989; United Nations, 1991).

Women's multiple roles

Throughout the world, most women do not have an equal share of land, credit, education, employment, and political power, in comparison to the men of their society. Yet, in every society, women play vital roles. In rural areas, for example, they perform the bulk of 'unpaid' and unappreciated household work, as well as contributing significantly to agricultural production. Approximately half the world's food is grown by women, and an estimated two-thirds of women workers in developing countries work in the agricultural sector (Power, 1992; Rhodda, 1991). Yet many governments (not to mention agencies such as the World Bank and the International Monetary Fund) assign little or no economic value to women's labour. Development planners generally assume that household heads are males, regardless of who is supporting the family. The result is that governments — made up almost entirely of men — have failed to integrate the value of women's work in their data-bases. Unless the HDI includes this critical variable, it will simply be repeating the errors, and producing skewed data. Women's participation in the service sector has expanded in many parts of the world, as has women's involvement in many informal sector activities; but once again the HDI fails to incorporate these variables.

Moreover, in many societies women have less opportunity than men to attend school; thus, although women make up half of the world's population, two-thirds of the world's illiterate are women. Denying females education has trapped generations in a cycle of illiteracy and poverty. Unless such forms of gender discrimination, not to mention violence against women (that begins in many societies with the practice of female infanticide), are incorporated within the HDI, a clear picture of human development, or the lack of it, will never emerge.

A gender-sensitive HDI

If the HDI is to be a realistic measure of human development, it must include women's vital contribution to development. The creators of the HDI must ensure that their data-base of critical indicators, such as employment, income, mortality, education, consumption and shelter, are disaggregated by sex. Their models must assign an economic value to women's unpaid domestic work, as well as their increasing under-paid and under-reported work in the formal and informal sectors. Only by drawing on the vast knowledge and experiences of women themselves, and including more women advisers and policy-makers on its staff, will the UNDP be able to develop a more gender-sensitive HDI, and thus a more effective measure of human development.

Shalendra Sharma lectures at the University of San Francisco. Contact: Department of Politics, 2130 Fulton Street, San Francisco CA 94117-1080. Tel: (415)666-6452; fax: 666-2772; e-mail: sharmas@cluster.usfca.edu

References

Boserup, E (1989) *Women's Role in Economic Development*, London: Earthscan.

Power, J (1992) *The Report on Rural Women Living in Poverty*, Geneva: International Fund for Agricultural Development.

Rhodda A (1991) *Women and the Environment*, London: Zed Press.

United Nations (1991) *Women: Challenge for the Year 2000*, New York: UN.

Interview

Magda Mateus Cárdenas

Director of Centro Amauta, Cusco, Peru

Interviewed by Caroline Sweetman

Magda, what is your history? How do you think your own life has affected your professional development?

My life has been influenced by circumstances, other people, and a multitude of challenges. I believe that in this I am similar to many women who have come from a less privileged background than mine.

In the 1970s, I was one of many young people of my generation who wanted change, and became politically active. I learned to read Marxist texts, and take a look at the reality of my country. I didn't have to go without food or housing, but I remember learning that there were many social and economic disparities in this country, that marked you out; they made one want to do something with one's life, in order to escape them.

In the 1980s I was the first woman to become president of the Centro Federado de Estudiantes de Antropolgía (Federation of Anthropology Students). Although I did not have what I would call a 'feminist perspective', I believed that we women, too, were capable of running things. We faced up to the challenge of proving that we were capable of doing more than domestic chores or working as secretaries, that we could conduct a political argument just like men could, we could formulate proposals, and engage in discussion with other people and negotiate with the university authorities to achieve our aims.

Can you give me an example of a particular event that was significant in your working life, which maybe helped to focus your interest in gender issues?

In the 1980s, I went to work for a rural development NGO. With one other female anthropologist and a female development worker, I was one of a team working with peasant women. Like many women development workers involved in this type of situation, we wanted to do what was best. The projects were aimed at women, seeking to improve their lives, to build up savings, to meet family needs, and to encourage women to participate in society. They were essentially well-intended, but often lacking in a political perspective. Through training courses in weaving, sewing, and market gardening, we were constantly seeking to develop women's organisational capabilities, with the aim of strengthening the ties of solidarity between peasant farmers.

In 1989, at the first conference of the National Rural Women's Network organised by the Flora Tristán Women's Centre in Lima, an event which brought together a large number of Peruvian development workers, we discussed the question of a 'methodology for working with women'. I, like many others, was resistant to the notion of a specific approach. We felt that in principle, development approaches should be valid for both men and women. Yet we recognised that some issues were of particular importance to women; one of the participants was Ximena Váldez, a Chilean feminist, who spoke about her work with women in her country. This had a great impact on me. I learned that it was necessary to take account of the issues of culture, class, and gender, in order to understand the lives and concerns of women.

On my return I began to look at women's lives in a new way, to find that peasant women, too, differed among themselves, that they had individual needs and demands. Since then, I have sought to document their reality and adopt a perspective of empowerment. Eventually I joined Centro Amauta, a feminist organisation, with which I still work today. The experience of the Amauta team was something new for me; it touched on many points I was not aware of previously, including sexual and reproductive rights, and the problem of violence against women. Over the years

that I have worked with the team, we have expanded our perspectives and our commitments, until we are now an organisation which is consulted on issues of gender, class, and culture at both national and regional level.

Most theories of organisational development emphasise that they are designed for men. Why are equal opportunities policies inadequate to address all concerns for gender equity?

Our societies are essentially structured on the basis of masculine power, and class- and culture-based intolerance. There are few opportunities for women to exercise power, and these are still being developed. Until now, there have been very few organisations headed by women, apart from women's community groups and feminist NGOs. Although women's professional abilities are recognised, it is very rare for them to be appointed to positions of responsibility.

As women, we want power; yet we would wish to transform it in accordance with our own values, based on solidarity, equal co-operation, and democracy. If we just take notice of equal opportunities, we don't think of transformation; we are often guilty of committing the same sins of concentrating power, acting in an authoritarian manner, and adopting a masculine attitude towards power.

Also, equality of opportunity at work does not operate in practice, because technical and economic considerations are seen as being much more important. Women themselves allow their own contribution to go unnoticed or, as generally happens, are almost always involved with the social aspects of the work, which are considered less important than the productive side, where achievements are quantifiable. Achievements on the social side cannot be measured until long after the event.

Since development workers are characterised as having a concern for social justice, do you think development organisations find it easier to address gender issues than commercial organisations?

Many men and women, inside and outside development organisations, have a concern for social justice. Yet this does not mean that development organisations are automatically able to recognise all aspects of social injustice, or to address them. The families with whom NGOs work are often viewed as neutral entities, without any differentiation as far as power is concerned. Also, there is often a prejudiced attitude to feminism, and to discuss women's rights is seen as a subversive act. There is considerable resistance to dealing with questions of this nature.

Many organisations have embarked on work with a gender perspective, without understanding its transcendental character. They assume that they are working in a gender-sensitive way because they take account of both men and women, but it is very rare for thought to be given to the political aspects of such a perspective, and their institutional aims seldom include political objectives.

What has been your experience of working to integrate women, and a concern for women's equality, into development organisations?

Funding agencies have encouraged some development organisations to work with a gender perspective through support procedures, internal workshops, the development of analytical procedures, and policy clarification. Results have been useful in some instances, but there has been resistance, insofar as it is seen as being a fad, imposed by the North, or by urban feminists. Often, an idyllic view is taken by funding agencies of the reality of

life in rural areas; there is much reference to the 'complementary relationship' between men and women, emphasising the role of traditions and culture, without much critical analysis.

However, there have been some examples of change from within. Organisations have undergone major changes; they have looked critically at their mission and their achievements, giving priority to self-education and staff training. These changes have taken place at different levels, often starting with a core group of development workers, male and female, with an awareness of the issue, or in other cases from above, initiated by senior management.

Generally, I see a concern on the part of development agencies to integrate a gender perspective, but in some cases it is regarded as just one more factor to be included in development projects, and is not regarded as a perspective which changes views of development itself.

How important is the issue of one's own identity in working on gender issues? Can male development workers behave as feminists? Conversely, can we assume that women will support gender equity?

These are important considerations. I believe that it is not enough for us as women simply to be aware of our rights; men have to recognise that we have them, and this is a task for men as well as women. It involves re-examining personal attitudes which go back years. I really do believe that if workers can learn how to become aware of their own masculinity they will be able to take the political demands of feminism on board. But this kind of thinking is recent, we have yet to see how successful male feminists will be.

As far as women are concerned, their level of awareness is greater because of their personal experiences; however, we should not forget that there are women who reflect 'macho' values, and others who allow themselves be carried away by a technically-oriented perspective, and ignore social issues.

What's more important: getting equal numbers of women and men at the top of organisations, or ensuring that those at the top — either women or men — have a vision of equality between the sexes?

I believe that it is important for us to have equality of access to power and decision-making as an ultimate objective. But it is also important for us to ensure that we have as allies to help us in the task of influencing other men and women, men who are themselves aware. Such men, while recognising the differences that exist between us, are able to construct a dialogue and create a climate of tolerance. We also need women with leadership and negotiation skills, who can give expression to a political discourse to explain our strategic interests.

How do you think development organisations can best work to promote gender issues in communities where the topic is seen as an attack on traditional culture?

In the mountain communities, little attention is given to the issue of culture. It is assumed that relations between men and women are based on complement-arity. It is argued that within the peasant family unit, everyone has their own contribution to make, and everyone has productive and reproductive responsi-bilities. The argument is a valid one, but we are unwilling to accept that it is appropriate to the reality of the peasant economy, where the family plays an important role as a unit of production and consumption, but is also the place where power relationships, identities and roles are constructed and assigned distinct social and economic values.

Consequently, it is important for development workers to be aware of these gender relationships, how they are constructed and how they manifest themselves. We cannot continue imposing our own prejudices on the world of the Andes, as though we were dealing with two self-contained or separate societies. They are a part of this country and are structured around social, economic, and historic institutions which are constantly renewing themselves and, like all others, capable of deploying power.

NGOs need to update their analyses, not simply for socio-economic and geo-graphical purposes, but more importantly to serve as ways of getting closer to the reality in which they seek to intervene. They also need to develop ways of system-atically organising their experiences and evaluating their actions. The continuous development of 'theory' and 'knowledge' should help in resolving dilemmas of long standing.

However, it is not always possible for these processes to be carried out indep-endently, hence the need for funding agencies to clarify policies and provide support and external monitoring.

Once all this is in place, I think that it will be easier to work with the com-munities themselves since the problems that we are referring to are not unknown to them; they are part of their everyday life, and should provide the basis for developing approaches for the raising of self-awareness, for men as well as women.

Do you use the language of 'feminism' in these communities?

There is a lot of stereotyping and prejudice where feminism is concerned. It is assumed to be the opposite of 'machismo'. What is important is how we work on the content and the political dialogue, and how we strive to ensure the visibility of those aspects of the female condition which go beyond the reality of women in poverty. The construction of citizenship, a sense of belonging, autonomy and empowerment, all have an important role to play within that subjective experience, because they are not issues divorced from daily life. What is important, therefore, is to achieve an identification with what it feels like to be a woman, and to develop methods of understanding and analysis which can be translated into action. This is not something that can be done overnight; it is a challenge for the medium term and the long term.

We have had very limited opportunities as far as the agencies are concerned. We have worked mainly through the gender interest group in Novib's Partners' Platform, and the same partners are also involved in efforts to bring influence to bear on other mixed partner agencies, who have not been working on the issue.

What is the most important issue for you to work on in your region?

Work must be done on the organisational, social, and political aspects of the theme of autonomy and empowerment, adapting the content and methods to reflect local circumstances. However, there is another topic that we need to tackle now: the development of management capabilities and skills, not just in relation to social matters, but to economic work as well. A precondition for women's emancipation is access to, and control of, financial and economic resources. An aspect of this, which has been ignored until now, is training in technical skills, and access for women to the marketplace on more competitive terms.

Training for women has almost always been provided in connection with domestic livestock production, market-gardening, and matters relating to family health care. Projects offering training for the work-force in the technical aspects of agricultural or industrial production are few and far between. This is an area which is generally reserved for men, ignoring the fact that women are also part of the workforce, and that investment in their training will reduce the technological, social, and power divide between men and women.

Magda Mateus Cárdenas is Director of Centro Amauta, Cusco, Peru. Contact details:
tel. 084-240572
e-mail: camauta+@amauta.rcp.net.pe

Resources

Compiled by Sara Chamberlain

Book Review

Gender, Culture, and Organisational Change: Putting Theory into Practice
Itzin C and Newman J (eds),
Routledge, 1995

Gender, Culture and Organisational Change consists of a collection of articles based on a decade of research and experiences gained from 'equalities work' in public sector organisations. Although most of the material in the book is drawn from experiences in Britain in the 1980s and 1990s, it makes wider connections with women and trade unions in Europe, and management development for women from the South. The editors have included a diverse range of approaches and methodologies, but there are both explicit and implicit connections between the chapters. Although gender relations in organisations are the primary focus, women are never seen as a homogenous group, and divisions based on class, race, and physical ability are also examined.

The main concern is with the need to change organisational cultures, structures, and practices, shifting the balance of power towards greater parity between women and men. The book argues that, before change can be brought about, gender-based inequalities in organisations have to be made visible, and that research is one of the most effective ways to achieve this. Case studies demonstrate how different research methodologies can be used to reveal, and help us to understand, gender relations in organisations. The studies also demonstrate how practice and experience can be used to inform and develop theory.

The book offers a number of theories about organisational culture, and develops several models of 'change strategies', based on insights gained from research experience. It then goes full circle by exploring how theories about organisational culture, change strategies, and the research process itself can be used to initiate change.

In the opening article, Janet Newman defines organisational culture in terms of shared symbols, language, practices, and deeply embedded beliefs and values. She considers organisational culture to be a site of conflict, not consensus; employees actively create organisational culture, rather than passively accept it. Newman emphasises that organisational culture is not integrated and undifferentiated, but multidimensional, and 'strongly divided along departmental, functional and professional lines'. Organisational cultures should be seen as fluid, active and changeable, rather than static.

In their article, Catherine Itzin and Chris Phillipson explore how men's and women's work chronologies differ, and how entrenched sexual stereotypes about gender and age disadvantage women. They base their analysis on a survey of 449 local authorities in the UK, plus 11 public-sector organisations, 3 private-sector companies, and an attitude survey of 476 local government line-managers.

Itzin and Phillipson argue that work is 'structured to accommodate a male chronology of continuous employment, not the female chronology, which combines child-rearing and domestic responsibilities and the discontinuity which involves moving in and out of paid employment'. While women commonly come into their 'golden work decade' in their forties, because of child-care responsibilities in their thirties, older women are very rarely promoted because 'they are seen by dominant organisational culture as ageing earlier than men, as becoming less responsible and capable, and more temperamental, as they get older — as past their "sell-by date" after forty'.

The second part of the book turns to the development and implementation of strategies for change, providing examples of initiatives related to gender and race in UK local government, in trade union activities in Europe, and in 'developing countries'. In Chapter 8, Catherine Itzin evaluates different models of 'strategic change,' arguing that the most useful are the ones which highlight 'the importance of leading people through the process of change, of targeting key individuals and enlisting their support, of overcoming resistance, and helping people to unlearn old ways and to deal with perceived threat, and real pain'.

Different diagnostic tools that can be used to develop change strategies include SWOT analyses, which involve identifying the strengths, weaknesses, opportunities and threats in an organisation; 'key relationship mapping', which can make it possible to identify 'the winners and losers in the change process, who had power in the organisation, and who had hard and soft information'; and force-field analysis, which identifies forces which promote and constrain change in organisations. Finally Itzin argues that change strategies should emerge in response to an evolving situation; change is 'not necessarily linear, deliberate, and continuous, but sudden and built on potentials that have been latent or peripheral in the organisation'.

Chapter 14, written by Gwendoline Williams and Marion Macalpine, demonstrates how the diagnostic tools outlined by Catherine Itzin can be used in conjunction with the concept of a 'gender lens' — gender analysis — to both 'surface' gender-based inequalities in organisations, and to craft strategies to change them. In 1991, Williams and Macalpine launched a management development programme for women civil servants from the South. The aim was 'to enable participants to intervene in the complex and unequal relations of power within public administration agencies, in the context of unequal north-south relations, and to increase women's access to and control over resources'. The programme targeted public administration, because gender-bias in administration was seen as one of the main reasons 'for the consistent failure to "integrate" women in development policy and practice'.

In the final chapter, Janet Newman writes that the 'challenge is to spot the trends, identify the spaces where change is possible, make the most of productive alliances, and mobilise resources and arguments that can help at that particular moment'. Newman emphasises that when crafting change strategies, we must be aware of the 'shifting political terrain'

outside our organisation. As the book's authors are quick to point out, gender-bias in society shapes and sustains gender bias in organisations, and organisational change can never be fully achieved unless gender bias in society is tackled.
Review by Sara Chamberlain.

Further Reading

'Gendering organizational theory', Acker, J, in A J Mills and P Tancred (eds), *Gendering Organizational Analysis*, Sage, UK, 1992.
Examines what is meant by 'gendered organisations', and the processes that reproduce power imbalances between men and women. Gives an overview of the development of organisational theory, and suggests that women feminist theorists are unusual in being simultaneously both inside and outside ruling structures. Emphasises the central role of sexuality in the reproduction of hierarchy and suggests how gender analysis can be a resource for organisational change.

Art of Organising Training Sessions, 'Thirty Tools on Diversity and Organisational Change', NGO Forum, Fourth World Conference on Women, Huairou, China, 1995.
Includes articles on how to analyse organisations, communication in organisations, leadership, 'the learning organisation', negotiation skills, diversity in organisations, gender policies, goals and actions, and power. Contains many useful checklists and practical guidelines that can be applied to gender and organisational change. Available in English, French and Spanish from Novib, Amaliastraat 7, The Hague, The Netherlands.

'Gender in institutions: an inward look', Barrig, M, in M Barrig and Andy Wehkamp (eds), *Engendering Development: Experiences in Gender and Development Planning*, Novib/Red Entre Mujeres, The Hague/Lima, 1994.

A Latin-American perspective on the institutional work of NGOs regarding gender. Ponders the old, but still pertinent question of whether it is necessary to create women's units in institutions wanting to take a gender-sensitive approach to their projects, or preferable to integrate planning that takes gender into account into broader activities. Focuses on NGOs that work for, and with, women.

Women in the Public and Voluntary Sectors: Case Studies in Organisational Change, Brown, H, Office for Public Management, UK, 1994.
Examines aspects of effective equal opportunities implementation in the public and voluntary sectors, focusing on the National Health Service in the UK, housing associations, and higher education. Develops a methodology to detect barriers to women's advancement. Suggests that a narrow focus on equal opportunities is ineffective without timescales, targets, and monitoring procedures. Sees a need to link changes in policies to initiatives that address organisational processes and culture. Concludes that equal opportunities policies in the 1980s underestimated the need for a pluralistic approach; the degree of resistance; the time-lag involved in change; the need for monitoring; and the need for equality issues to be understood as intrinsic to management processes.

'From the woman's point of view: feminist approaches to organization studies', Calas, M B and Smircich, in Clegg et al. (eds) *Handbook of Organization Studies*, London, Sage, 1996.

In the Way of Women: Men's Resistance to Sex Equality in Organizations, Cockburn, C., Macmillan, 1991, USA.
Based on research that evaluates how men sometimes help, but more often de-rail or resist, feminist change in four large

organisations. Shows how women as a sex, but also black people, lesbians and gays, and people with disabilities, are compelled to hide their 'difference' if they wish to claim equal rights. Also looks at how these different identities interact with hierarchies of class. Formulates a counter-strategy for transformative change in organisations that involves acknowledging and asserting bodily and cultural specificity.

Managing to Discriminate, Collinson, D, Knights, D and Collinson, M, Routledge, London.
Argues that despite post-war changes in gender relations in the UK, occupational segregation by sex persists in the labour market. Criticises traditional Marxist-feminist theories of gender inequality in the labour market for neglecting human agency, but draws heavily on their concern with asymmetrical power relations. Uses empirical material to illustrate how job segregation is reproduced, rationalised, and resisted in the recruitment process. Case studies focus on the banking, mail-order, food, and manufacturing industries. Prescribes some organisational changes necessary to eliminate sex discrimination in the recruitment process.

'Gender and Administration', Goetz A M (ed), *IDS Bulletin* 23/4, 1992.
Argues that public administration is in itself a process that promotes the interests of men. Questions the idea that women's lack of privilege is an outcome of the operation of 'neutral' forces and institutions like the market. Develops the outline of a theory of gender in organisations, central to which is the dynamic interactions between gender relations within social relationships and within organisational relationships in public administration. The main conclusions are that mere tinkering with structures, procedures or representative bureaucracy is not adequate to challenge power systems.

Also that gender and transformative bureaucratic change cannot occur independently of a political context supportive of women's empowerment. *IDS Bulletin* is published four times a year by the Institute of Development Studies, University of Sussex, Brighton BN1 9RB, UK.

Speaking Out, Breaking In, Goetz, A M (ed), Zed Press, forthcoming.

A *Best Practices for Gender Integration in Organisations and Programs*, Hamerschlag, K and Reerink, InterAction Community, March 1996.
The results of a telephone survey of 30 member agencies, including CARE, Oxfam America, Save the Children, and World Wildlife Fund, regarding their efforts to integrate gender concerns into programming and internal management policies, and to learn about the 'best practices' of member agencies on a wide range of gender issues. Issues surveyed include: family-friendly work policies, gender and recruitment policies, proportion of women to men in senior management positions, and gender policy development and programme planning.

Institutionalising Gender Perspectives and Gender Training: The Experience of the Asian Pacific Development Centre, Heyzer, N, APDC.
Charts the history of the Women and Development Programme, and gender policy at APDC. Includes sections on 'Establishing our identity and work methods', 'Strengthening our case,' and 'Changing organisational culture'.

Instraw News: Women and Development No 17, on 'Women and Management', 1992.
Examines the status of women in 'decision-making' bodies (government administrations, organisations) in Africa, Asia and the Pacific, China, Latin America and the Caribbean, and Europe. Available from INSTRAW.

Managing Diversity, JAMLC.
A monthly source of information, ideas, and tips for people managing a diverse workforce. Available from: JALMC, P.O. Box 819, Jamestown, NY 14702-0819, USA.

'A development agency as a patriarchal cooking pot: the evaporation of policies for women's advancement', Longwe, S H in *Women's Rights and Development: Vision and Strategy for the Twenty-first Century*, Oxfam Discussion Paper 6, 1995.
An entertaining and instructive demonstration of how the failure of gender policies to be implemented in the North is closely mirrored by a similar 'evaporation' of policy in Southern development administrations. Looks at the mechanisms and procedures by which this evaporation takes place, and concludes that bureaucracy is not gender-neutral; it is the means by which patriarchy preserves the existing power relations that govern development co-operation.

Gender Planning in Development Agencies: Meeting The Challenge, MacDonald, M (ed), Oxfam, UK, 1994.
Includes thematic papers and case-studies from organisations such as Oxfam, ACTIONAID and HIVOS. Keynote papers cover areas such as gender-aware planning and institutionalising gender. Provides a thorough overview of the main issues arising from the workshop, in areas such as policy, institutions and partnership.

Gender Policy and Black Holes: Some Questions about Efficiency, Participation and Scaling-Up in NGOs, Mayoux, L, Open University: UK, 1994.
Looks at recent trends in NGOs towards efficiency, professionalism and scaling-up, and the restructuring involved in achieving these aims. Explores some of the possible implications of these changes, and argues that unless women's empowerment is taken seriously in its own right,

and authoritative institutional frameworks put in place for implementation, then gender policy risks falling into a series of 'black holes' within and between these wider NGO aims.

'Power, institutions and gender relations: can gender training alter the equation?' Murthy, R K, Unpublished paper, 1995.
Discusses the strengths and weaknesses of gender training as a strategy for altering equations of power within oneself and institutions. Identifies NGOs as 'gendered' entities, and argues that the manner in which women and gender ideologies have entered organisations reflects and perpetuates gender hierarchies in society. Available from Gender and Programme Learning Team, Policy Department, Oxfam, 274 Banbury Rd, Oxford, OX2 7DZ; please enclose a stamped addressed envelope.

Guidelines for Good Practice in Gender and Development, National Alliance of Women's Organisations (NAWO), 1993.
These guidelines aim to promote good gender practices in development agencies, and solidarity and educational organisations. Include guiding principles for staff, volunteers, and management.

Gender, Power and Organisations; A Psychological Perspective, Nicolson, P, Routledge, 1996.
Examines the psychological consequences of gender imbalances in work organisations for senior and middle-ranking women. Argues that although there are more senior women in organisations today, these increased opportunities have not been gained without psychological consequences. Examines how patriarchal structures hinder women's progress, and how success in the world of work has psychological implications for women's sense of subjectivity, self-esteem, and gender identity. Also examines the

impacts that achieving against such odds has on women's everyday lives.

Gender Responsible Leadership: Detecting Bias, Implementing Interventions, Nostrand, C, Sage, 1993.
Analyses how we all consciously or unconsciously assist in upholding a culture that tolerates male entitlement, privilege, and violence. Aims to help us become aware of sexism in ourselves and others; to promote gender-fair intervention strategies; and to create learning and working environments that are equally supportive to men and women.

'Mainstreaming Gender in Organisations', Oxfam Gender Learning Workshop reader, Oxfam, UK, April 1996.
A collation of articles about 'mainstreaming' gender in organisations. Available from Gender and Programme Learning Team, Policy Department, Oxfam 274 Banbury Road, Oxford OX2 7DZ, UK.

Feminist Policy Advocacy: Transforming International, National and Local Development Institutions, Razavi, S. and Miller, C. (eds), UNRISD, Geneva, forthcoming.

'BRAC Gender Quality Action Learning Program: Evaluation Design,' Rao, A and Kelleher, D, Draft Paper, June, 1995.
Describes how evaluation methods were developed to gauge the success of organisational learning process on gender in a development NGO in South Asia. The evaluation looked at the outcomes and impacts of the gender programme on staff knowledge and skills, and on organisational and programme quality. It also examined the programme's strengths and weaknesses; the causal factors that led to change, or a lack of it; and changes that needed to be made to the programme. Describes a participative action-learning process through which these changes could be made.

Power and Process, Reardon, G, Oxfam 1995.
Discusses Oxfam's experience of integrating gender issues into its programme and organisational structure. Includes five papers on major issues facing gender and development practitioners, including Florence Butegwa on the law, and Lori Heise on violence against women.

Breaking with Tradition: Women and Work, The New Facts of Life, Schwartz, F, Catalyst, 1992, USA.
Explores major issues facing women and families in the 1990s. Discusses ways for both employers and employees to manage the issues surrounding maternity, methods for institutionalising flexible work arrangements, and employing and encouraging women capable of leadership.

'Making differences matter: a new paradigm for managing diversity', Thomas, D A and Ely, R J, in *Harvard Business Review*, September–October 1996.

Anthropology of Organizations, Wright, S (ed), Routledge, 1994.
Five essays on gender and organisational change. Brings together anthropological studies of the complex ways in which people make and contest meanings in organisational settings. Critically examines the organisational culture concept, from an anthropological perspective. Explains the embeddedness of gender relations, and shows how — despite widespread change — inequalities persist, using case studies from government organisations, private companies and a union.

Printed in the USA
CPSIA information can be obtained
at www.ICGtesting.com
JSHW072020140824
68134JS00041B/3720